The Kalem Players in front of Jacksonville's Vim Theatre in 1910.
Florida Photographic Collection, Tallahassee, Florida.

The First Hollywood

Florida and the Golden Age
of Silent Filmmaking

Shawn C. Bean

University Press of Florida

Gainesville Tallahassee Tampa Boca Raton
Pensacola Orlando Miami Jacksonville Ft. Myers Sarasota

12 11 10 09 08 6 5 4 3 2 1

Library of Congress Cataloging-in-Publication Data
Bean, Shawn C.
The first Hollywood : Florida and the golden age of silent
filmmaking / Shawn C. Bean.
p. cm.
Includes bibliographical references and index.
ISBN 978-0-8130-3243-6 (alk. paper)
1. Motion picture industry—Florida—Jacksonville—History.
I. Title.
PN1993.5.U73B43 2008
791.4309759'12—dc22
2008002685

The University Press of Florida is the scholarly publishing agency for the State University
System of Florida, comprising Florida A&M University, Florida Atlantic University,
Florida Gulf Coast University, Florida International University, Florida State University,
New College of Florida, University of Central Florida, University of Florida, University
of North Florida, University of South Florida,
and University of West Florida.

University Press of Florida
15 Northwest 15th Street
Gainesville, FL 32611-2079
www.upf.com

For Maw and Paw,
who pushed me in the right direction
and Brandy,
who kept me going that way

Contents

Acknowledgments

When assembling a book so deeply rooted in the past, it's at times impossible to touch, see, or (in my case) hear your subject matter. As a result, a lot of help was needed to create the story's road map. Many hours were spent in archives, libraries, and film centers around the country, each providing links to people long passed and places long gone. Eileen Brady at the University of North Florida's Thomas C. Carpenter Library helped me sort through old texts and copies of the *Florida Times-Union*, *Florida Metropolis*, and *Jacksonville Journal*. Charles Silver, director of the Museum of Modern Art Film Study Center in New York, is a walking encyclopedia of film history. He was critical to the book's execution. The Richard Norman Collection at Indiana University's Lilly Library was an essential source, and Rebecca Cape, head of reference and public services, made sure I found what I needed there. Paul Heyde, head archivist at the Black Film Center/Archive in Bloomington, Indiana, holds several Richard Norman films and screened them for me. Neal "Adam" Watson at the Florida Photographic Collection of the State Archives of Florida helped me locate most of the visuals. Lydia Stewart at the Ritz Theatre & LaVilla Museum was kind and forthcoming with information about her historic institution and put me in touch with other contacts in Jacksonville. Another key source, Todd Roobin of the Jacksonville Film and Television

Office, should be commended for modernizing the way the city promotes and attracts new film and television projects. The Jacksonville Historical Society's extensive holdings have overtaken its small space at Jacksonville University. Sharon Laird managed to find every surviving newspaper clipping, brochure, image, and handwritten note relating to the city's film history.

There are also the people who took time to chat with me about their connection to Jacksonville's film industry, past, present, and future: Richard E. Norman, Jr., who was so gracious, is making his father's private world accessible; Ann Burt, the caped crusader who helped save Norman Studios; Devan Stuart, head of the Norman Studios Silent Film Museum; Todd Roobin; Holly Keris at the Cummer Museum of Art and Gardens; Jacksonville architect Robert Broward; Lisa Bradberry; Herman McEachin; and Richard Alan Nelson, whose *Florida and the American Motion Picture Industry* was my own version of the King James Bible.

Speaking of writers, many thanks to those who helped build the foundation of this book: Wayne Wood, Robert Broward, Eileen Bowser, John Cowart, Thomas Cripps, Richard Fleischer, Richard Fogelsong, Gary Mormino, Michael Newton, Lewis Jacobs, and Robert Sklar. Special thanks to Scott Eyman, author of *Lion of Hollywood* and *The Speed of Sound*, for offering such great advice to a rookie writer, and Patrick D. Smith, author of *A Land Remembered*, who made me fall in love with this complex and stunning state.

Thanks to friends and colleagues who supported me creatively prior to this project and during its execution: Thomas Chilcoat, my West Coast correspondent; and Esther Jackson and Phyllis Pesaturo, whose own passion project, *Florida International Magazine*, gave me a platform to do what I love. And of course, special mention to those instrumental in making *The First Hollywood* a reality: John Byram, editor-in-chief of the University Press of Florida; project editor Susan Albury; copy editor Kate Babbitt; and my agent Frank Weimann at the Literary Group International.

Family and friends also deserve a moment on the marquee. Their love and encouragement was constant long before any of this book stuff came about: Brandy, Jackson, and Tanner; Garnet and Scarlett Bean; Aaron Bean; Susie and Gary Baxter; Stevie, Melissa, James, and Isabella Henderson; Hardee and Geralynn; Chip Smith; Hugh Smallwood; Deme Mekras; Marian Lloyd; the Bledsoe family; and Stanley Bean.

One hundred tellings are not so good as one seeing.

—Chinese proverb

THE First Hollywood

Introduction

Circle of Faith Ministries is a two-story structure with small picture-frame windows. It is the whitest, brightest building in Arlington, a post–World War II suburb of Jacksonville dominated by mechanic garages, auto detailing shops, and car washes.

Inside the church, nine brass chandeliers hang from the ceiling, providing the majority of the sanctuary's light. The congregation files in for 11 a.m. worship, and they're surprisingly casual. There are sweatshirts, T-shirts, and Miami Heat jerseys but also the occasional eggshell four-button suit and hibiscus-sized brooch with colored gemstones.

The three-hour service never takes a breath—even when things quiet down for a moment, the white noise from the synthesizer's amplifier fills the room with an audible buzz. The morning begins with forty-five minutes of hand-clapping, savior-shouting praise, followed by a skit announcing the week's scheduled activities, more praise, tithing, PowerPoint slides that project scripture on the wall, and a rousing sermon by Pastor Joseph McRoy. It's the type of dramatic, electrically charged service that would make an atheist wonder if the Holy Ghost is more than just adrenalin and answered prayers more than just coincidence.

Many of these churchgoers don't know that nearly a century ago, this building was home to its own version of drama. Where there are now chairs, hymnals, and banners of scripture (the one behind the pulpit is from Romans 8:31: "If God be for us, who can be against us"), there were once Klieg lights, spools of celluloid, and artificial backdrops. This was the indoor set building for Norman Studios, one of the thirty-plus film studios that populated Jacksonville during the early twentieth century. As it happens, the Circle of Faith congregation is largely African American, and Richard Norman, the namesake of the film studio, was a white filmmaker who produced black-cast films for black audiences.

But this story goes much deeper. To talk about Jacksonville is to talk about Metro-Goldwyn-Mayer (MGM), Fox Broadcasting Company, Oliver Hardy, D. W. Griffith, Mary Pickford, the Barrymore family, and the advent of Technicolor. Approximately 300 films were produced in Jacksonville from 1909 to 1926. This was no one-off pit stop. The city was *this close* to becoming the country's premier destination for movie production. It's not that hard to imagine. Jacksonville is plenty big enough to accommodate everyone—at 841 square miles, it is the largest city in the United States. It offers warm weather and beautiful tropical surroundings, a huge plus if you were a movie producer who lived in the frigid corridors of New York or Chicago, where all the money was at that time. Unfortunately, a number of issues collided and tore it all asunder: greed, world war, racial strife, health epidemics, the judging eye of moral reformers, and under-the-table politics. But the biggest obstacle of all was That Other Film Town.

By sheer coincidence, the above-mentioned visit to Circle of Faith Ministries took place on the same day as the 79th Annual Academy Awards. As these words are being written, Ari Sandel is taking the stage to accept the Oscar for Best Live Action Short. His film, *West Bank Story*, is a farcical musical that trades Jets for Jews and Sharks for Palestinians. Since 1927, the Oscars has been the annual tribute to the world's most popular trade; more than one billion TV viewers tuned in to watch the event in 2007. And the glitzy affair has always taken place in Hollywood, the movie industry's mining town. The professionals live in Santa Monica, act in studios in Burbank, edit in the offices of Universal City, promote at Grauman's Chinese Theatre on Hollywood Boulevard, and take home golden statuettes down the block at the Kodak Theatre, the regal 3,400-seat venue adorned with cherry-wood balustrades and silver leafing. These locations are part of a world-famous constellation, connecting the city like the stars in Orion's sword.

To see Hollywood's role in moviemaking and Jacksonville's disconnect from it, one only need watch the Academy Awards. As the West Coast town is mentioned over and over like a Best Actor nominee, Jacksonville is nowhere to be found. The first and only time Jacksonville had anything to do with the Oscars was in 2002, when *Murder on a Sunday Morning* won for Best Documentary. Not that the city has much to be proud of: produced by two French filmmakers, *Murder on a Sunday Morning* chronicles the story of Brenton Butler, a sixteen-year-old black youth who was falsely accused of and tried for murder. According to the documentary, the Duval County police beat the confession out of him.

Hollywood wasn't always a monopoly. The title *The First Hollywood* is no hyperbole: the first Jacksonville studio predates the first permanent West Coast studio by three years. In fact, the year of this book's release, 2008, marks the 100th anniversary of Kalem Studios' arrival in Jacksonville.

For a brief time Los Angeles and Jacksonville, locales with very similar geographic and meteorological DNA, competed to be America's filmopolis. Now huge studios and Beverly Hills mansions populate the former and decaying warehouses and weathered marquees litter the latter. Looking at it today, it's hard to believe this former cattle crossing in North Florida was once a destination for the booming silent film industry. It's like telling someone that Wall Street used to be in Oklahoma's Tornado Alley, or Da Vinci's *Mona Lisa* was originally exhibited at Machu Picchu.

The First Hollywood shares this untold story, piecing it together using old newspaper clippings, autobiographies of filmmakers, library archives, first-person interviews, and second-hand accounts. But Jacksonville's silent film industry also requires a look at Jacksonville itself: its history, social and racial makeup, and civic catastrophes. While these issues might seem random or immaterial, the city's backstory—which includes civil war, segregation, and city-ravaging fires—served as content for the city's directors and screenwriters. These were the earliest days of narrative fictional filmmaking, and Jacksonville's past was a source of inspiration time and again. Conversely, these issues helped define the most necessary cog of moviemaking—the audience—and producers catered to their tastes and prejudices. As a means of comparison, the book also keeps tabs on Hollywood: its beginnings, progress, failures, and accomplishments. This is, quite literally, the tale of two cities.

During Pastor McRoy's sermon, he repeatedly mentioned a snippet of scripture from I Peter: "Ye are a chosen generation, a royal priesthood, a holy nation." The Oscars is, or at least wants to be, a pageant of the royal, the chosen. To think there was a time when the crown was up for grabs.

❧ 1 ❧

New Year's Day, Twentieth Century

We sat there with our mouths open,
without speaking, filled with amazement.
—Georges Méliès

On the morning of January 1, 1900, residents of Jacksonville picked up copies of the *Florida Times-Union* and saw the headline "Welcoming the New Year" in dense, inky sans serif type. Flanked by other headlines about the war in Samoa and the session of Congress the following Wednesday, "Welcoming the New Year" was a call to arms for a country advancing at a staggering rate. Even more apropos for this nation of industrial workers, the New Year rang in on a Monday morning.[1]

Inside the *Florida Times-Union*'s first edition of the twentieth century was a column dedicated to the progress of these United States of America. "The people who lived at the beginning of the 19th century had no railroads, no telegraphs, and no newspapers worth mentioning," the author writes. "They were ignorant of the sewing machine, and had no concept of the telephone. Of course, they knew nothing of the great variety of modern electrical inventions, which have so much to do with what is now regarded as ordinary comfort." But in spite of the writer's hyperbole, this was still a nation in its infancy. The national debt was a mere $2.14 billion.[2]

Outsiders seeking a glimpse of modern America in 1900 could peek in on New York or Chicago, cities so advanced they could have gotten their first tonnage of brick off the Niña and Pinta. However, if you wanted to see civic possibility in a Petri dish, there was no better example than Jacksonville, tucked into the nape of a peninsula that dangled like fishing lure over the Caribbean. It was already a city of massive sprawl, a trait that continues today. At the turn of the twentieth century, Jacksonville was a low-rise cityscape; church steeples and ship masts were the defining postcard features until City Hall's Mediterranean clock tower and the U.S. Courthouse and Post Office arrived in the 1890s.

According to the U.S. census, the population in 1900 was 28,429. There were wealthy neighborhoods (Springfield to the north, Riverside to the southwest) and poor neighborhoods (the Hansontown slums). Although it suffered from the typical discrimination of the era—schools, theaters, restaurants, hospitals, trains, and churches were segregated—Jacksonville was surprisingly progressive in its racial and social makeup. In fact, 57 percent of Jacksonville's residents were black, and within that group a considerable middle class had formed. According to the *Jacksonville Directory for 1900*, the black professional community included 131 businesses (including groceries and laundries, shoe repair shops, and barbershops), sixty-nine teachers, forty-nine ministers, six doctors, three lawyers, and one pharmacist. Wealthier black Jacksonvillians built homes in the neighborhoods of Oakland and LaVilla, only a stone's throw from Forsyth Street, home of the white glove set.[3]

Women were no less active. One-third of all women in Jacksonville were employed. They worked as waitresses, secretaries, laundresses, and servants but also as ministers, physicians, and journalists.

While on paper these facts would seem ideal for a Chamber of Commerce brochure, let's not forget they were living in a country still idealistically flawed. Women's suffrage was still two decades away. Despite the Emancipation Proclamation, blacks were living in a world of prejudice thinly disguised as law. During elections, angry mobs on horseback swooped through town to keep black men from the polls. "Black codes" were enforced throughout the South. In Florida, a former slave could be hanged for burglary, poisoning, and attempted rape (death was assured if the victim was white). Blacks could not use "abusive or provoking language" toward whites. A common misdemeanor punishment was thirty-nine lashes and an hour in the pillory. Whites suffered nothing similar when they were convicted of the same crimes. And why should they? Hadn't they suffered enough? Decades after Appomattox, Dixie's pride was still an open wound. Sadly, living under the Black Codes was much better than the rogue justice practiced regularly by the hooded ghouls on horseback, hopped up on bigotry and charcoal whiskey.[4]

Jacksonville was the rook on Dixie's chessboard: deep, deep, deep in the corner. But that position came to influence much more than just racial and social constructs. What ignited this city's boom was that it was part of the south, not part of the South. Unlike most destination cities, including Newport, Rhode Island, considered the dandiest vacation spot on the eastern seaboard, Jacksonville was a warm tropical mecca—an estimated 15,000 visitors spent the entire winter in Jacksonville. On New Year's Day 1900, the news dailies in the north were reporting the effects of a severe nor'easter that had hit Boston and shut down the shipping harbors. Meanwhile, North Florida was enjoying one of its mild winter days (average temperature: 60 degrees), which made open-air horse-drawn cabs the transportation of choice.

As a result of the growth in tourism, a slew of proper hotels was built in the second half of the nineteenth century. Jacksonville hospitality began conservatively with the Judson House, built in 1853. The 110-room structure had 136 feet of frontage along Bay Street and broad verandas that lined the first and second floors. A mob of men burned it down less than ten years later—unfortunately, fire is a prominent and recurring theme in Jacksonville's history.[5]

The era of Florida's grand Gilded Age hotels arrived with the St. James Hotel, built in 1869 along a considerable stretch of Laura Street. The pet project of two capitalists from Boston and Connecticut, the St. James was built for $30,000 and featured accommodations for 500, hot and cold baths, a bowling alley, and a billiard room. Word of this grand hotel spread fast among the nation's haves. In 1874, poet Sidney Lanier described an evening at the Jacksonville inn: "The chances are strong that as one peeps through the drawing room windows on the way to one's room, one will find so many New York faces and Boston faces and Chicago faces that one does not feel very far away from home after all."[6]

While it sat at the head of the table, others quickly joined the St. James: the Everett, the Duval Hotel, the Oxford House, and the Carleton. And of course there was the Windsor. Inside were anterooms, dining rooms, and accommodations for 200 guests. The long veranda, prettied up with hanging flower baskets and decorative arches, surrounded the hotel like a picture frame. The veranda was an ideal place for guests to lounge in rocking chairs and look out over Hemming Park. The St. James and the Windsor were the alpha and omega of Jacksonville's considerable inventory of luxury inns. Dukes and U.S. presidents, Vanderbilts and Rockefellers were often listed in their guest registries.[7]

So what was it about this city, really? Granted it was warm, but warm wasn't always an easy sell. At the time, doctors believed that the warm climate bred yellow fever and malaria—quinine pills could often be found in the pockets or purses of those heading into this questionable frontier. In contrast to other warm locations, Florida was promoted as a home for the ill, an alfresco sanitarium. In 1875, Joseph Howe wrote *Winter Homes for Invalids: An Account of the Various Localities in Europe and America Suitable for Consumptives and Other Invalids During the Winter Months.* He suggested St. Augustine, due south of Jacksonville, as a great place for invalids and their families but recommended staying in a private residence because "the old hotels . . . generally lack all the requisites of a healthy residence, and, unless they are improved, should be shunned under all circumstances."[8] Business was also part of Jacksonville's attraction—shipping and agriculture were two industries creating its economic base. But what made the city special? What *made* the city? What was its trademark, its postcard centerpiece?

America has always had a soft spot for river cities. Perhaps it was Mark Twain's *Huckleberry Finn* and its narrative conduit, the Mississippi River ("a whole mile broad, awful still and grand") that cemented this sentiment. New York is flanked by the Hudson and East Rivers. The Chicago River runs straight through downtown; in 1900 the river's flow was completely reversed, making it both a natural wonder and one of the Industrial Age's greatest hits. St. Louis was nicknamed "River City." For years rivers entertained the country's aristocracy, providing boundaries that separated accents and class hierarchies. A river can make a city full of brick-and-concrete stoicism live and breathe.

The St. Johns River, the only river in the country that flows north, was the scene of Jacksonville's birth. It is 310 miles of anecdotes and recollections. It is a story of Paleo-Indians, Protestant reformers, Spanish conquistadors, Carolina slaves, British occupiers, Confederate deserters, and Yankee capitalists. Like some sort of primordial evolution, what later became

Jacksonville crawled from the shallow basin of the St. Johns onto dry land. Millennia later, the city would employ the river as its center-ring attraction.

❧ ❧

Five million years ago, after the glaciers melted and water levels began to even out, the tidal lagoons, marshes, bluffs, and embankments of the St. Johns River Valley took shape. The Atlantic Ocean had swallowed the St. Johns whole for eons, eventually spitting it out so it could become its own rolling entity. The St. Johns was first a crossing for Late Pleistocene–epoch herds of mammoth and bison, which would wade through the brackish waters and wander about the salt marches, pine hammocks, scrub oak woodlands, and flatlands dotted with magnolia, cabbage palm, and gum trees.[9]

Paleo-Indians and Archaic Indians were the first human settlers to occupy this territory, setting up villages along the riverbanks 16,000 years ago. They hunted deer, fished for freshwater snails, and picked berries from the nearby forest. Their dead were buried along the river, the bodies wrapped in grass and bones and then interred at the water's edge.

The Timucua Indians are largely considered the first residents of the St. Johns River Valley, mostly because they were the first to encounter European settlers, the self-appointed authors of history. The Timucua were a mythical, shamanistic, superstitious people. The men's bodies were tattooed with decorative bands and half-moon blades inked on their legs and torso. Their religion was a mix of magic, weather, fashion, and flora. Lightning was a premonition of war; fires were started to ward away evil spirits. They cut their hair to signal distress, often instigated by the death of a loved one.[10] In addition to farming, hunting, and warring with other nomadic tribes, they herded cattle. Driving the herds across the river led to Jacksonville's first name. The shallow embankment was named "Wacca Pilatka," translated from Timucua as both "cow ferry" and "place of the cow's crossing."

But this history was largely lost once white people arrived. Easter Sunday, 1513, fills Chapter 1 of American history textbooks. It was the year made famous by Juan Ponce de León, the Spanish explorer who landed north of Canaveral and south of Pablo Beach (Ponce de León officially recorded his landing as 30 degrees and eight minutes latitude). When he later described his arrival, Ponce de León said that "the land was fresh with spring and the fields were covered with flowers." This new land's name was all about timing;

for the Spanish it was Pascua Florida, "Flowery Easter." With a simple beach-
ing of their ships (and permission from King Ferdinand, of course), Ponce de
León claimed the peninsula for Spain.[11]

The Spanish maps of the new land prominently feature the St. Johns; it
cuts across the cartographs like the slash of a knife. The river is titled Barra de
San Juan.

It was the Timucua, the true residents of the river basin, that could have
recorded the comings and goings of the white men who claimed ownership
of their land. Sadly, they became spectators of their own lives. The spring of
1565 was the last time Timucua were seen in the St. Johns River Basin. It is
believed that the Europeans pushed them deep into the forest, where star-
vation and disease took their toll. By 1728, the Timucua were considered
extinct.[12]

Florida was a bargaining chip as kingdoms and empires positioned for
dominance. If you passed through Cowford (a British bastardization of the
translation of "Wacca Pilatka") during the summer of 1821, you likely trod
on both Spanish and American soil. Florida was transferred to the United
States that July. With this announcement the city was surveyed and streets
were named (Liberty Street and Washington Avenue as patriotic odes; Forsyth Street for General John Forsyth, U.S. minister to Spain, who negotiated
Florida's acquisition). The city's first laws were written ("any person or persons bringing beef, pork or mutton, to sell at the public market . . . shall ring
the bell at least one minute before exposing the same for sale").[13]

One last time the town needed a new name. Unanimously the residents
chose Jacksonville, after General Andrew Jackson, Florida's territorial governor who had been born near the border of the Carolinas. Jackson's renown
came in waves, first as the hero of the Battle of New Orleans, then as president of the United States, an office he would take only seven years after his
surname was bannered across a North Florida cattle town. His presidency put
the city's name in lights, or at least in oil lamps.

Jacksonville's modern ascent arrived via the narrows of the St. Johns. In the
late 1820s, steamships from the north imported everything from cotton to
timber to indigo to turpentine; it was also a regular stop on the trade express-
way between Manhattan Island and the West Indies. By 1850, Florida had
entered the Union, and as a housewarming present the federal government
gave it half a million acres of public land.

Then one day in 1860, the boom ceased. Word was that LeMat revolvers and Springfield muskets were trading fire at Fort Sumter in Charleston. No one died during combat, but one man, Private Daniel Hough, was mortally wounded when a gunpowder keg ignited from a stray spark. It was the first casualty of the American Civil War.[14]

Now the St. Johns carried not promise but demise. Union gunboats arrived at the mouth of the river only days after Mayor H. H. Hoeg told locals that "it is useless to attempt a defense of the City of Jacksonville."[15]

Old Hickory's town was occupied four times during the Civil War. By the summer of 1864, the city had witnessed the bloody Battle of Olustee, when downtown (six blocks, twenty-five buildings), seven sawmills, four iron foundries, a railroad depot, and an estimated four million feet of lumber were burned.[16] Throughout it all, the St. Johns was indiscriminate, a friend to both blue and gray, peace and death.

To reignite the economy after the war, the St. Johns was dredged. At its prewar depth of ten feet, the largest tugboats and steamboats would have carved up the riverbed, their hulls like the business end of a hatchet. In the fall of 1870, 15,000 cubic yards of sludge was removed, and in 1898, a retaining wall was built to preserve a depth of eighteen feet.[17]

Just as "by sea" was being checked off the to-do list, "by land" was waiting for its upgrade. For years Jacksonville was the last major train stop on the southern rail line. But that changed with the arrival of Henry Flagler, who not only opened all of Florida to travel but also made Jacksonville the hinge of the state's social and commercial activity.

Henry Morrison Flagler, one of the preeminent twentieth-century businessmen, was born in Hopewell, New York, near the Finger Lakes. Like many others of the era, Flagler's first business partner was John Barleycorn: his rookie hustle was selling whiskey for six cents and beer for thirteen cents a quart. Instead of serving in the Civil War, he bought canteens for the soldiers.

Flagler's business grew to include the grain trade, which brought him into contact with a young entrepreneur named John D. Rockefeller, a connection that led to Flagler's partnership in Standard Oil. The company was the prototype for a monopoly; publications such as *McClure's*, an early template for in-depth journalism and muckraking (put the *Atlantic Monthly*, the *New Yorker*, and *Time* into a blender), often used its pages to skewer Standard for poisoning the free enterprise system. Through oil refineries and the ever-consolidating northern railroad systems, Standard grew to become the unrivaled alpha male of U.S. industry. By the 1880s, Flagler was obscenely wealthy. With his gray hair parted with pomade, walrus mustache swallowing his upper lip, and three-piece suits enveloping his stooped frame, he was the epitome of the nouveau riche American businessman.

Flagler came to Florida, more specifically St. Augustine, in December 1883 with his second wife Ilda Alice Shroud. In Jacksonville Flagler saw "the Newport of the South." He was fond of giving cities nicknames with the catchy gloss usually reserved for advertising copy—he would later dub Palm Beach "the Queen of Winter Resorts," Miami "the American Riviera," and Key West "America's Gibraltar."

Flagler's first order of Florida business was building his own Gilded Age establishment. The Ponce de León Hotel, completed in 1886, was a Moorish fortress covering four and a half acres. In front, two towers and their terracotta balconies, each weighing five tons, overlooked the sprawling courtyard and gardens. Out back, Flagler built studios for the local artists.[18] There was also a marketer inside that pinstriped suit. In 1890, Flagler sent word of the first coast up the East Coast by distributing 25,000 brochures to northern hotels and advertisers. He licensed an image of the Ponce de León to a Jacksonville cigar company, which used the grand hotel on its packaging.

Jacksonville and St. Augustine were making strides, but they were anomalies in this new frontier. The poor whites still lived in squalor, Indians hid in the scrub oak and pond cypress, and malaria and yellow fever thinned the population. To the south, the Seminole Wars raged on the flats of Key Biscayne. Key West was still half a century away from becoming a Caribbean-flavored tourist town for coeds on spring break and fishermen who nicked their sea tales from Hemingway.

In 1885, the Jacksonville Railway gave one of the richest men in America a free travel pass. The company was wooing Flagler in the hope of employing his business acumen. When the railway named him to the board of directors, it won him over. On New Year's Eve 1885, Flagler bought a $300,000 stake in the Jacksonville Railway. Soon after that he began the long and tedious process of accumulating the state's railways: the Jacksonville, St. Augustine, and Halifax Railway; the St. Johns; the St. Augustine and Palatka.

Along these new routes Flagler built and bought passenger depots, hospitals, hotels, and schools. He added stations in up-and-coming coastal cities such as Daytona Beach, which would later gain fame for its car races on the hard-packed sand (the course was best at low tide). Flagler's Florida East

Coast Railway (FECR) kept heading south. As thanks for connecting them to FECR's southern line in 1896, South Floridians wanted to name their new boomtown after Flagler. He declined, recommending the town stick to its old Indian name, Miami, the Seminole word for "that place."[19]

As Flagler's rails burrowed south, eventually crossing 128 miles of the Florida Straits to reach Key West, his contributions to Jacksonville quickly became footnotes. But his influence should not be overlooked. It was Flagler who put the first bridge over the St. Johns, which was originally intended to direct passengers south to his St. Augustine hotels but instead funneled people into Jacksonville. He also built the Jacksonville Terminal, making it the cynosure for Florida travel. This huge hub was the eye of a spiderweb; parallel bars of steel headed in every direction, from Palatka to Yulee to Tampa to Palm Beach to Daytona.

By the late nineteenth century, Jacksonville was known as the "Winter City in Summer Land." From 1882 through 1887, there were 272,343 winter visitors in Jacksonville, a staggering number considering that the city's year-round population was a tenth of that figure. Faced with declining tourism, California began a campaign in 1888 to steer tourists from Florida to the Golden State. It was the first competitive challenge between Florida and the West Coast. But not the last.[20]

❧ ❧

California had much to overcome. For the major metropolises of the time—New York, Boston, Providence and Chicago among them—California was a world away, a cross-country train ride where travelers could expect several sunrises and sunsets before finally huffing the Pacific's salt air. Even more daunting was the lingering lore of the Wild West, a place immortalized by dime-store novels. The Gold Rush, Wild Bill Hickok, Calamity Jane, the James Gang, and Deadwood, South Dakota, were the stars of a tourist's quest for adventure.

Meanwhile, Jacksonville was doing just fine entertaining the crowds, which consisted of dignitaries from New York and London, European royalty, honeymooners, literary celebrities, and bohemians. They often congregated along Bay Street. There you could browse shops selling alligator-teeth whistles, heron plumes, and palmetto hats. Over by the docks and harbors, you might find a live alligator tethered to a bulkhead.[21]

Social engagements in late nineteenth century Jacksonville consisted of camping by the river (known as "marooning") and all variety of outdoor functions (barbecues, picnics, and such) and dances (square, Spanish, waltz, etc.). After the war, entertainment developed into a grand spectacle. On Talleyrand Avenue, there was the Ostrich Farm, a regular advertiser in the *Florida Times-Union.* "Nearly 100 Giant Ostriches, standing 8 to 10 feet high, weighing 250 to 400 pounds each," read one ad. "Ostrich Nests, Eggs and Baby Ostriches only a few days old." The fine print mentions that electric cars ferried between downtown and the Ostrich Farm every fifteen minutes.[22]

There were also sports and the arts. In 1883, Jacksonville hosted the championship Greco-Roman wrestling match between Thiefaud Bauer and D. C. Ross. That same year, the first baseball club was founded. Years later, the New York Giants made it the site of their spring training. The Park Opera House, a 1,200-seat hall built of heart pine, opened in 1884 with an inaugural performance of *Faust.* Packed houses showed up for performances of *La Traviata, The Mikado,* and *Il Trovatore.* Three years later, the building was destroyed by fire and was rebuilt with brick.[23]

California continued to threaten Florida's tourism. The state offered discounted railroad rates and opened tourism offices in Florida to feed locals pro-California literature. Jacksonville took a preemptive strike to ensure its entertainment value: it built America's first theme park, the Sub-Tropical Exhibition. Its aim: to promote the benefits of tropical life—the people, products, and resources of Florida, Mexico, Central America, the Bahamas, and West Indies. A huge exhibition hall was erected, a 50,000-square-foot monolith with glass windows the size of Rembrandt's *The Night Watch* and striped towers with pointed turrets—a train station with hallucinogenic sheen. When it opened on January 12, 1888, visitors could view large stands of fruit, indigenous jewelry, tonics, and elixirs, all displayed under streams of Spanish moss. The take for the four-month event was $21,013.[24]

There was plenty of room for sports, opera, square dances, tropically themed spectacles, and so forth because film was still something of a ghost. At that time, film was closer to science than entertainment—making pictures move was more akin to reversing the flow of the Chicago River than to mounting *La Traviata* at the Park Opera House.

꿍 ꂃ

Persistence of vision is defined as the holding of an image in the mind's eye until the next image arrives to take its place. The brain is not a recorder of events but a perceiver of them. For example, for the color-blind individual, blue may have always been green; it is not automatically registered as blue because Moses Harris's color wheel labeled it so. In the mind, successive images are not recorded but created.

Scientists say persistence of vision is a myth; film academics say it's a theory. Either way, it is this mental process that makes motion pictures possible. Like a magician's sleight of hand, motion pictures tickle a physiological phenomenon. It's an otherworldly obliteration of this-worldly limitations.

There were many early attempts to exploit persistence of motion, some perhaps never recorded by history. One of the earliest and most influential to later inventions was William George Horner's zoetrope: a cylinder with evenly spaced slits, its interior lined with sequenced images. As the cylinder spins, a look through the side created the illusion of rapidly moving successive images. Other inventors, from fields ranging from photography to astrophysics, would add their own twists and tweaks to the zoetrope.

Identifying the father of modern-day film has everything to do with time and trust: when did it happen, and do you believe the source? The three film forefathers most celebrated today were working on separate continents but no doubt in competition.

Although responsible for the incandescent light bulb, the phonograph, and the telephone transmitter, Thomas Alva Edison didn't like being called "the Wizard of Menlo Park." The term *wizard* implied his work had something to do with magic; he wanted people to realize that his accomplishments were the result of arduous unrelenting hard work, not some virgin birth of imagination. Edison had conquered sound, but he wanted sight to go with it. It's no coincidence that his first image recorder was fashioned from the parts of a phonograph.

German Ottomar Anschutz's devices inspired Edison, namely the cylinder of photographic plates where each picture is captured by a Geissler tube flash. The Geissler tube could illuminate and extinguish like a crude strobe light. Edison took his own ideas, borrowed from Anschutz, and after a few takes settled on a moving image maker: a cylindrical drum that was fed celluloid strips of photographic emulsion. The strips, provided by Edison acquaintance and photography technician John Carbutt, were simply scraps—Carbutt was trying to make unbreakable glass by covering it with sheets of celluloid. He gave the long bands cut from the windows' edges to Edison. It would be an historic exchange, as the shape of film stock would never be altered or modified.[25]

The first film shoot for the newly named Kinetoscope took place in 1888, starring the slapstick comedy of Edison's mechanic Fred Ott. Most famous of the day's shoot: Ott's sneeze, now held in the Library of Congress. Donning a necktie and meat cutter's smock and holding a white handkerchief in his right hand, Ott rears back and fakes a sneeze, then breaks the fourth wall with a sly grin. It is largely held that those films, dubbed the "Follies of 1888," were history's first motion pictures.

Across the Atlantic, two French brothers were inspired and challenged by Edison's creation. They were Auguste and Louis Lumière (as fate would have it, *Lumière* is French for "light"). These scientists wanted to improve the Kinetoscope, which lacked one of film's definitive qualities: there was no projection. To view Edison's early films, you had to place your eye on a small viewfinder that magnified the celluloid. They were the original peep shows. A small oversight on Edison's part made it possible for the Lumières to reimagine the Kinetoscope without copyright infringement. On August 24, 1891, when Edison applied for a U.S. patent for his film device, the clerk suggested that Edison pay extra to cover its foreign patents.

"How much will it cost?" Edison asked.

"Oh, about $150," the gentleman said.

"It isn't worth it," said Edison.

An empire lost in an instant.[26]

So the Lumières went to work on their own version—a suitcase-sized camera, processing center, and projection machine all in one—dubbing it the Cinematograph. The most significant alteration was the addition of a claw mechanism, similar to the mechanism that moved fabric on a sewing machine, that advanced the film by pulling down on the stock's sprocket holes.

Although Edison had recorded motion pictures years earlier, the Lumières' first exhibition at the Salon Indien at the Grand Café in Paris is the birthplace of modern cinema. It was Christmas Eve 1895. The room was dressed up exotically with bamboo and elephant tusks on the walls. The evening was much like a cocktail party, although it wasn't without its Hollywood premiere pizzazz. Outside the Grand Café, a carney shouted, "Come in, ladies and gentlemen. Come see the cinematograph of the Lumière Brothers of Lyon! For only one franc, you'll see life-size figures move and come to life before your very eyes." The Lumière brothers didn't even attend. [27]

The first thing the crowd saw was an image of a horse and buggy frozen on the wall. This picture, sadly, had no motion. The audience grew restless. Then suddenly, amazingly, an industry was born.

In attendance that night was Georges Méliès, a magician, theater manager, and future father of narrative filmmaking. He relayed his reaction: "No sooner had I stopped speaking when a horse pulling a cart started to walk toward us, followed by other vehicles, then passers-by—in short, all the hustle and bustle of a street. We sat there with our mouths open, without speaking, filled with amazement."[28]

The reaction was overwhelming. Inquiries came by the bushel about purchasing the Cinematograph, including one from Edison himself. The Lumières responded with a succinct, emotionless form letter that must have seared the famed inventor.

> Thank you for your letter. Our new invention, the Cinematograph, is currently under construction in Paris and we are not yet in a position to say when it will be on sale. Nor are we able yet to determine what the sale price will be. As soon as this information is in our possession we shall forward it to you.
>
> Yours faithfully, A. Lumière[29]

⁂

Film arrived in Jacksonville in the summer of 1897, less than two years after the industry's official genesis. The Park Opera House, dedicated to the performing arts, gave this crude bumbling art form its debut. Even more interesting is that the film wasn't even an original. It was a remake.

Enoch Rector and Samuel Tilden, two producers from the tiny Latham Film Company in New York, knew the country had a love affair with prizefighting and more specifically for champion and pugilist hero "Gentleman" Jim Corbett. The two decided to film a fight between Corbett and challenger Bob Fitzsimmons. The match took place in Carson City, Nevada, and Rector was prepared to record the event, equipped with three Veriscope cameras and 48,000 feet of negative. For twelve rounds the two Irish fighters delivered blows and drew blood. Rector exposed 11,000 feet of film. The film was first screened in New York, where the *Brooklyn Eagle* reported that "the man who would have predicted, at one time in our history, that an event of a prior month would be reproduced before the eyes of a multitude in pictures that moved like life . . . would have been avoided as a lunatic or hanged as a wiz-ard."[30]

But Rector and Tilden encountered obstacles that would later plague gen-erations of filmmakers: censorship, piracy, licenses, and distribution rights.

In Philadelphia, Sigmund Lubin was advertising his own film, *The Great Corbett-Fitzsimmons Fight*. How could this be? Was he a rogue, a fink, a capi-talist? All three, it appears. While Rector and Tilden's film was caught in a web of legalities, Lubin hired two freight handlers from the Pennsylvania rail terminal to reenact the prizefight. The blow-by-blow commentary, pulled from a local newspaper's account, was read simultaneously.

The film was first screened at the Park Opera House on July 2, 1897, using the Edison Projectoscope. Every one of the 1,200 seats was filled. Halfway through the film, the stock broke in half. The mishap portended this city's future with film: exhilarating, action-packed, fleeting.

A City Burns

Was there no end to this calamity?
—Benjamin Harrison

This is the point in the movie where everything changes. It's the plot device that appears early in the first act and, when detonated, turns everything on its head, instigating a shift that powers the rest of the screenplay. A husband is found cheating, war breaks out, children are kidnapped, a last will and testament uncovers a $100 million inheritance. The plot device for the city of Jacksonville comes and goes like quick hell. It wipes the slate clean, and even though Jacksonville's story is already millennia old, it begins again for the first time.

Florida was flourishing in 1900, a steamroller of a state raising eyebrows above the Mason-Dixon. In his 1901 book *Acres of Ashes*, Benjamin Harrison described the state's growing economy:

> Down on the long peninsula crawled trains that labored with the weight of tourists returning to the north and west after a winter which had filled every hotel in the land to overflowing and gladdened the hearts of the landlords. . . . In orange grove and pineapple plantation, on truck farm and tobacco field, laborers appeared and the work of the day began.[1]

Nowhere was Florida's ascent more evident than in Jacksonville. With the population now at 30,000, it was a city full of industry and amusement. A steady stream of Clyde Line steamers pushed up the St. Johns. Henry Flagler was busy constructing his latest hotel, the Continental Hotel, in nearby Atlantic Beach. Gala Week, a parade filled with firefighters, police, floats, and revelers, began on November 26. There was a golf tournament at the country club and a circus performance near the Union Railway Station. Built in 1897 and accented with a tile roof and decorative arches, it was the largest railroad terminal in the South.[2]

Residential neighborhoods were thriving. Riverside was the most picturesque of them all, a modern-day Beverly Hills where the ornate homes were upstaged only by the names of the wealthy living behind the wrought-iron gates. Wellington Cummer, the lumber magnate, lived in a huge white-washed mansion with a two-story columned entry, wraparound porch, and two chimneys. Dr. Abel Seymour Baldwin, one of the city's best-known surgeons and physicians (and for a long time the city's *only* surgeon and physician), resided in a massive home with verandas on the first and second floors; it looked like it had escaped from the French Quarter of New Orleans. Most Riverside architecture leaned toward Gothic Revival and Queen Anne: gingerbread-style façade details, Corinthian columns, asymmetrical towers and turrets that seemed to have been attached at the last minute.

Fire was not uncommon in Jacksonville. The combination of southern heat, minimal firefighting resources, and a slew of buildings made from wood—live oak, pine—made the young city vulnerable. In 1854, a spark drifted from the steamship *Florida* and landed on a hay shed. It quickly ignited and over the next five hours fire consumed fifty buildings, homes, and businesses. During the Civil War, fire was the favored artillery of the blue and gray. The biggest blaze the city endured occurred on March 29, 1863, a gift from the Union troops. "Spanish moss, dropping so gracefully from the avenues of splendid oaks, has caught fire," wrote one New York newspaper. "As far as the eye can reach, nothing but sheets of flames can be seen, running with the rapidity of lightning."[3]

These became footnotes on Friday, May 3rd, 1901. This blaze would forever be spoken in the same breath as the Great Chicago Fire of 1871, which caused $200 million in property damage and left 98,000 homeless, and the San Francisco Fire of 1906, which destroyed a staggering 28,000 structures. Boston and Baltimore also suffered from wanton fires.

In Jacksonville, Edward E. Cleaveland was owner and manager of the

Cleaveland Fibre Factory, a bedspring and mattress company in LaVilla, a largely black neighborhood close to the Hansontown slums. The company's main occupation was making mattress fiber from all varieties of natural materials: cured feathers, palmetto leaves, and Spanish moss, which Cleaveland employees plucked from the trees using long poles. On that fateful day in May, the workers had laid a pile of Spanish moss to dry outdoors on a wooden platform about 200 feet square.

A stone's throw from the factory, a pine shanty's chimney caught fire. A small ember from the chimney drifted over and landed on the platform of drying moss. Most of the employees were off that day, and the ones on the clock—a few mattress workers and upholsterers, an elderly seamstress who'd been with the Cleaveland family since the days of slavery—were nestled in the moss taking an afternoon nap, a practice not uncommon after lunch.

The tiny bonfire caught the eye of one of Cleaveland's employees. He sounded the alarm, and workers dumped bucket after bucket of water on the fire. It was a small fire with heavy smoke—all bark, no bite. It did little to portend what was to come.

Suddenly the wind picked up. Clumps of burning moss flew about like tumbleweeds. The Cleaveland Fibre Factory was the first victim in their path. With its pitch pine frame and wooden shingles, it took to the blaze like a fish to water. The wind continued, and within minutes many of the Hansontown shanties were a hot mess.

12:35 p.m.

Once the Cleaveland Fiber Factory's roof caved in, its contents—fiery bits of moss, feather, and horsehair—rose from the pyre, swirling in the breeze and scattering about the city.

12:50 p.m.

For the residents of Jacksonville, curiosity turned to concern and anxiety. "The streets were filled with the shrieks of women and of men who strove to comfort or guard them from the effects of their frenzy—through the crowds hurrying horses raced."[4] The Jacksonville Fire Department was completely outmanned. Fire Chief Thomas Haney had collapsed from smoke inhalation and exhaustion. An SOS was sent out to every neighboring city.

1:00 p.m.

Up until this point the fire was largely a nightmare for the city's most poverty-stricken residents. Hansontown, now nothing more than an outdoor furnace, had spit out its residents in droves; they drifted in packs away from the blaze, material possessions in hand. LaVilla was suffering a similar fate; curtains lapping outside the windows of homes became nothing more than a trap for wayward sparks.

Moving at a breakneck pace, the fire headed east toward the white, the wealthy. It consumed the mansions on Church and Laura Streets and the businesses of Bay Street. It hit churches, stores, and government buildings, one block methodically after the other: Main, then Ocean, then Newnan and Market Streets. Dynamite and ammunition shops exploded. Some fleeing residents stacked belongings at the foot of the Confederate statue in Hemming Park, as if the trickling fountain, or an allegiance to Dixie, would somehow save their family photos and jewelry boxes from incineration.

2:45 p.m.

Next came the obliteration of Jacksonville's chief attractions: those grand old hotels. The fire swept down Hogan Street, where the Windsor Hotel, which had become an impromptu safe house for refugees, lay directly in its path. "Into the hotel many had carried the goods saved hitherto, furniture and books had been piled in the halls—it was crowded with guests." Once the flame caught its façade, "a mass of humanity struggled and surged into the street and parted like waves of the sea as each followed its own judgment. . . . Was there no end to this calamity?" The wooden structure disappeared into the black billows and reappeared as only a charred skeleton.[5]

The St. James Hotel, directly across the street, was the next to go. Because it was closed for the season, it went down alone. In describing the fall of the two hotels, Harrison wrote, "Then the great Windsor and St. James . . . radiated heat far and wide, the flame of their burning ascended to heaven and they groaned with thunderous voices in their agony." Watching the same scene unfold, the *Florida Times-Union* wrote that it was "a searing typhoon of smoke and dust."[6]

In the late afternoon, the fire raced up to the shores of St. Johns. The smoke slid across the cool, smooth waters, swallowing those who had retreated by boat. Water moccasins killed by the heat floated to the river's surface.

7:00 p.m.

The wind finally subsided. The Market Street Bridge over Hogan's Creek was a narrow chute for the mass exodus—a "jam of humanity made the passage like that of swimming against the tide." With the balusters of the bridge quaking, the anxious crowd shuffled forward. "Exhausted, one would drop a burden and another would take it in turn for a rod—one would take a child from its mother's arms and proceed until a wave in this sea of humanity would force the two apart—then the mother's voice of fear would add a new terror to the scene."[7]

8:30 p.m.

The final flames were under control.

It was a hot, swift destruction. Rooftop photographs taken in the days that followed show a dusty line separating the Jacksonville that was—green grass, intact structures—from the Jacksonville that wasn't—bare, spindly trees and scorched, ashy earth. The images look like Pompeii: pillars and chimneys once attached to churches and homes now stood alone. The City Hall clock tower, once the highest peak in Jacksonville, was a brick entryway belted by rubble.

The Great Fire of 1901 destroyed 466 acres. A total of 2,368 buildings were leveled: ten hotels, including the St. James and the Windsor; twenty-three churches, including St. John's Episcopal Church; the cultural halls on

The charred remains of Jacksonville after the Great Fire of 1901. The fire leveled 466 acres and 2,368 buildings. *Florida Photographic Collection, Tallahassee, Florida*

Forsyth, including the Park Opera House; and Riverside's most revered residences, including the Elks Club headquarters in the former home of Dr. Abel Seymour Baldwin. A third of the city's residents, about 10,000 people, were homeless. Amazingly, only seven perished.[8]

On the morning of Saturday, May 4th, the *Florida Times-Union* met its readership with the following headline: "Jacksonville Devastated by a Most Destructive Conflagration." It stated that the city resembled "Jerusalem when taken by Vespatian, Rome set on fire in Nero's time, or Moscow by the Russians."

"An Awful Visitation," read the *Florida Metropolis's* top headline from that same day. Underneath it: "The Worst Calamity That Ever Befell a Southern City Strikes Jacksonville Yesterday and Thousands of People Are Homeless and in Want."

Even though ominous hints of the tragedy had already headed north—the fire's glow was seen from as far as Savannah; the trail of smoke all the way to Raleigh—confirmation of Jacksonville's destruction quickly reached up and down the eastern seaboard. On Monday, President McKinley sent a telegram from Washington, D.C., reading: "I have just learned of the calamitous fire that has swept over the city of Jacksonville and hasten to express our deepest sympathies. In common with our countrymen, I feel for those who have suffered."[9]

Journalist and humorist H. L. Mencken, the star of the *Baltimore Morning Herald,* was sent to report on the fire's aftermath. In his 1934 autobiography *Newspaper Days,* Mencken wrote, "When I arrived by train, all set to load the wires with graphic prose, there seemed to be nothing left save a fringe of houses around the municipal periphery, like the hair on a friar's head."[10]

Within the nothing Mencken saw much was happening. The homeless pitched cavalry tents. The streets were jammed with soldiers—the Governor's Guards from Tallahassee, the Columbia Rifles from Lake City, the Jacksonville Light Infantry—who enforced the martial law Governor W. S. Jennings had declared. They set up checkpoints armed with cannons and Gatling guns. Even the saloons were forced to stay closed; there would be no escaping the calamity in the bottom of a bottle. The *Jacksonville Journal's* interview with Mayor J. E. T. Bowden on Wednesday offered a somber view of all that was happening. "Jacksonville can keep the wolf away from the door for three or four days longer with the provisions that are here and on the way," Bowden said. "God bless the great heart of human charity that has heard our appeal for aid."[11]

The fire brought on a thousand new worries. The people faced crime, disease, homelessness, and unemployment. The *Florida Metropolis* reported that "there are a number of victims of the fire developing signs of insanity today, mostly females of delicate health who have nothing left."[12] But other worries were old, this disaster only amplifying them. The fire was supposed to be blind to color and class; the *Savannah Morning News* reported that "the disaster has effectually obliterated the dividing line between the rich and poor, and a common catastrophe has made all akin."[13] In fact, the city's racial divide had been exposed, not obliterated. Desperation and panic were key ingredients for a Molotov cocktail of racial paranoia. On Saturday morning, when Governor Jennings declared martial law and called in the state militia, he did so partly because of his belief that the black population, homeless and hungry, would resort to looting, vandalism, and violence. Revealing his racism, Benjamin Harrison wrote after the fire subsided that "the softest cheek ever nourished by Caucasian blood seems yellow and drawn under the firelight—the blackest African flushes into saffron and the eyes emit a gleam that seems borrowed from the cat's eye or the angry panther's."[14] Later, in relaying the reaction of the citizens, Harrison wrote of the "storm of sobs . . . loud and deep or piercing with savage notes from the African. 'Bress de Lawd, dis am de day of judgment!' shouted a religious enthusiast."[15]

As Mayor Bowden pleaded for help to the *Jacksonville Journal*, the nation was mobilizing. The Sunday after the fire, the New York Chamber of Commerce and the Merchants' Association of New York formed the Jacksonville Relief Committee; it immediately held a fund-raiser that yielded $22,000 and trainloads of food and clothing. The organization also helped with sanitation. It provided 127 toilets. Concerned that yellow fever would break out like it did in 1888, sanitation workers rounded up countless loose animals: hogs, chickens, turkeys, rabbits, coons, and mules. Forty states as well as England, Canada, and Cuba contributed $224,913, along with countless train cars stocked with supplies.[16]

However, not all of the help was helpful. Some cities didn't seem to understand Jacksonville's quasi-tropical locale or the fact that it had just been fried in a blaze: Montgomery, Alabama, sent a huge box of woolen mittens; St. Paul, Minnesota, contributed fur coats; Boston sent oil stoves. According to Mencken's autobiography, "The boys at the Pimlico racetrack contributed 100 second-hand horse blankets, and on the heels came one reporting that the saloonkeepers of Baltimore matched them with 100 cases of rye." A subsequent trainload of goods from Baltimore was slightly more appropriate: bales of splints, two gallons of sulfuric ether, a half-ton of bandages, twenty coffins, and a crate of wooden legs.[17]

No matter how relevant (or not) it was, relief came in droves. On Tuesday, a stretch of twelve freight cars came bearing 16,000 pounds of cornmeal, 15,875 pounds of ground coffee; 9,681 loaves of bread; 1,030 dozen cans of corned beef; 1,085 cans of baked beans; 6,000 sides of bacon; 900 suits for men, boys, and children; 870 dozen pairs of women's hose; and 1,088 pairs of shoes. The commissary handed out more than 200,000 food rations.[18]

Even as the hungry were fed and dead animals buried and the disorderly arrested, the half-burned city was open for business. Telegraph poles were replaced and repaired immediately; new wire was stretched across the streets. Employees of the trolley car company cleared the tracks and hung fresh feed wire. The post offices and Western Union telegram stations were operating as normal. Long lines formed at the lemonade stands. West Bay Street, Jacksonville's tourist center, was largely untouched. The stores on Bay Street were opened. Men were seen entering the stores without shirts or hats and leaving with new installments of Sunday best. Church congregations gathered under shade trees. The Church of Immaculate Conception set up under a tent; lumber draped across paint cans doubled for pews, pine boards for an altar.

Clean-up crews picked up debris and trash. They were also under orders to collect and save any loose bricks. They were to be used again.

⁂

It's now the second act of the movie. Everything has changed, and those at the crossroads of the plot have to find a new way. A fierce baptism has given Jacksonville a blank slate. And starting with those loose bricks, the city is being rebuilt.

At 10 a.m. on Monday, May 6, building permit No. 1 was issued to Rudolph Grunthal. He asked to build a temporary shack at the corner of Main and State Streets. That same day, the owners of the Windsor Hotel announced they would build bigger and better. About a week later, a new hardware store—100 feet square—had already been built and stocked with $39,000 worth of merchandise. By the end of 1901, building permits for permanent structures represented half the number of buildings destroyed by the fire.[19]

The stories of the Jacksonville fire, carried by headline and second-hand gossip, brought many thoughts to the nation's curious. Concern, certainly. Charity, naturally. But most embraced opportunity in the aftermath. The city worked hard to draw new businesses and entrepreneurs. An editorial in the *Florida Metropolis* gave the cause words, asking those holding land to "do the city and themselves the justice of naming a reasonable price for their property."[20]

Henry Klutho learned about the fire in the *New York Times*. The paper arrived at his office in Manhattan, which was the latest stop in Klutho's career. He had been raised in Breese, Illinois, inspired in St. Louis by the buildings of famed Chicago architect Louis Sullivan, and educated and trained in New York. He traveled to Europe to study and sketch the Beaux-Arts structures that were en vogue at the time. The 28-year-old was a stately looking gentleman known as "Jack" to his friends. Although his nose and ears were prominent, you were drawn to his intense eyes, which were known to inspect each tiny nuance of a schematic. In photos, his eyes were hooded by a strong brow.

In the summer of 1901, Klutho moved his practice to Jacksonville, accepting the city's open invitation to architects. He partnered with J. W. Golucke, a well-established architect from Atlanta. The two set up shop in a residence at 222 West Adams Street, where Klutho also slept.

The first commission for Klutho & Golucke was the Dyal-Upchurch Company building for a Georgia lumber and turpentine firm. Because its products were ideal for a city being rebuilt, the company moved to Jacksonville and bought a downtown parcel at 4 East Bay Street. Klutho's design called for a Second Renaissance Revival structure made from Indiana limestone and granite-colored brick. With a repetitive pattern marked by cubed windows, the structure was a subtle nod to Sullivan's Wainwright Building in St. Louis. Completed in May 1902, it was downtown Jacksonville's first high-rise. In fact, the sixth floor was added during construction because demand for the building was so high. Roughly 60 percent of the office space had been rented halfway through construction.[21]

The Dyal-Upchurch building was Klutho & Golucke's last commission, a turn of events that did nothing to abate Klutho's solo career. His commissions compounded at an extraordinary rate. The next major project was the residence of T. V. Porter, a prominent businessman who wanted to build on an elegant stretch of Church Street. This time Klutho reinvented colonial, giving the home a colonnaded veranda, three chimneys, and a grand portico with six Corinthian columns and an ornate coffered ceiling.

Klutho's inauguration as the city's definitive architect officially began on November 3, 1901, when the *Florida Times-Union* published the winning design for the City Hall competition. Once again, Klutho showed his versatility; the *Florida Times-Union* wrote that his plans "are in the style of the modern French Renaissance—perhaps the most popular style with the prominent eastern architects."[22] Klutho's City Hall is best described as Beaux-Arts, the European style with a proclivity toward the symmetrical and sculptural. Completed in 1903, the H-shaped structure was built of cream-colored brick and marble and crowned with a copper-capped octagonal dome forty feet in diameter. Inside, Klutho commissioned four murals by New York artist John O'Neill, each depicting a different aspect of Jacksonville.[23]

With hints of Realism, Renaissance, and Rococo, the murals were like something a modern artist would have created for St. Peter's Basilica. One of the murals was titled *Rebuilding*. Klutho's 1905 company brochure described it: "*Rebuilding* represents Jacksonville inspecting plans for the rebuilding of the city." Jacksonville, depicted as a woman in a flowing gown perched on a stone throne, is both Lady Justice and the virgin mother, the great overseer of the city's future. She is flanked by four men. "The engineer, rod in hand, stands in readiness to survey the site," wrote Klutho. "The mechanic seated on a broken and blackened capital, and the laborer, with his wheelbarrow, mattock, etc., are waiting the word to begin their labor. In the background is . . . the glow of the dying flames of the fire which devastated and destroyed 'old Jacksonville.'" But Klutho failed to mention the last man, who stands to the left of Lady Jacksonville, the plans for City Hall rolled out in front of him like a scroll. It is Klutho himself.[24]

What most benefited the city was that Klutho's tastes were never static.

His early European influences almost came to a screeching halt in 1905 after meeting a Chicago architect named Frank Lloyd Wright, whose Prairie School aimed not only to bring an organic, scaled-back sensibility to architecture but also to create something uniquely American in a field ruled by Germans, Italians, and Frenchmen. Klutho's short encounter with Wright left an indelible impression on his creative thought. The St. James building, Klutho's Prairie School monolith built atop the ashes of the St. James Hotel, was completed in 1912 and stands as his career-defining design.

Klutho's artistry inspired a renaissance and turned the city into an art gallery: during construction, many buildings placed their schematics in the windows for public review. But Klutho was only part of the city's promise. Handfuls of architects had come from across the country. Rutledge Holmes came to Jacksonville from Charleston shortly after the fire and was quickly commissioned for the new Duval County Courthouse and the armory, which faced each other like massive chess pieces across Market Street. A month after the fire, J.H.W. Hawkins arrived from New York. Although he lacked formal architectural training, he designed many of the grand residences in Springfield and Riverside. Also from up north was Wilbur Camp Bacon, who arrived in 1901. He was less than admired by his colleagues. His reputation was that of a snake oil salesman; he carried around a suitcase full of plans for sale.[25]

There were others, too. Ransom Buffalow from North Carolina preferred the gingerbread esthetic of Victorian homes. Mellen Clark Greeley's first project in Jacksonville was a bungalow at 2651 Oak Street. He would go on to co-found the Florida Board of Architecture. Earl Mark came from Demseytown, Pennsylvania, in 1901, and apprenticed under Klutho six years later. After moving from Ocala to Jacksonville in 1902, Roy A. Benjamin became the architect of entertainment, designing theaters like the Imperial, Palace, San Marco, Riverside, and Arcade as well as serving as associate architect for the Florida Theatre.

Something happened as these men applied their trade atop ash and ruin. The city became a patchwork quilt of styles. On East Adams Street, you could find Mission style at the Central Fire Station and Neoclassical Revival at Klutho's Public Library. The Church Street churches were Gothic and Romanesque. The neighborhoods of Riverside and Springfield exemplified the design schizophrenia. The Tudor homes were quaint. Georgian Revival and

Victorian residences built charm out of red brick. The Queen Anne dwellings, all spires and turrets and verandas, were shingled sandcastles. León Cheek's Jacobethan Revival residence at 2263 River Boulevard seemed to be trimmed in icing.

The first studio back lot had been built.

It was an inadvertent accomplishment that helped fuel the city's impending film boom. Filmmakers arrived here for the sunny weather, only to find that Charleston, Chicago, St. Louis, Atlanta, and Boston were available for the backdrop. And there was the St. Johns, still unchanged, which could double as the Mississippi, the Amazon, and the Nile.

⛧

When the Florida State Fair opened in Jacksonville in the fall of 1901, one of its most popular attractions was a tour of the city's burned district. By trolley the visitors shuttled through the hallowed site, framed by the St. Johns to the south and Hogan's Creek to the east.

How tacky, you may think. To offer a tour of this scabbed cityscape, to gasp at the grotesque, is in such bad taste. It's reasonable to think this way, and had the city still been in mourning, still been waiting for a miracle, it would have been no different that rubbernecking in Gibsonton, the village near Tampa where the Ringling Bros. circus freaks—the Siamese twins, the dwarves, the bearded lady, and the lobster boy—wintered during the off season. But Jacksonville was not interested in sympathy. Long before that first trolley headed into the fringe of LaVilla, a new boom had begun.

On December 14, 1901, Mayor Duncan Fletcher wrote an essay for the *Florida Times-Union*. "In the rush of things now making for the New Jacksonville, there is no time to stop or talk or write. Everyone is busy. . . . By six in the morning we begin to hear the saw and hammer, the passing wagons and drays, the foreman calling out his directions, the workmen responding in good cheer, the steam derrick and hoist starting the day's labor, and except for a short intermission for dinner, this continues until night."[26] In a report to the Jacksonville Board of Trade, Charles Smith wrote, "The truth of the matter is people here have been too busy to think about blowing their own horn. When you have a matter of 455 acres to cover with buildings of the best modern type, and only a few months to do it in, there is no spare time to devote to telling the world what a deuce of a fellow you are."[27]

New buildings replaced old buildings, replaced traces of the past. The Cleaveland Fibre Factory rebuilt on its old site. The city had learned its lesson; these structures were built for the future. Those old hotels built of pine and oak were nothing more than luxurious piles of kindling. The new structures were slate and stone and brick and marble, ready to resist any future drifting embers.

The Florida State Fair was not the only entertainment in the rebuilding city. The Labor Day parade filled the downtown streets with the heroes of the aftermath—carpenters, plumbers, longshoremen, railroad yardsmen, and stevedores—who processed in hordes to the Confederate statue in Hemming Park. That same month, the Ostrich Farm reopened, the birds relocated from their summer digs in Atlantic City. Amateur football teams made up of soldiers from the Jacksonville Rifles and Jacksonville Light Infantry scheduled home games against Georgia Tech and South Carolina College.[28]

Tourism returned as well. The new Windsor Hotel opened a year after the great blaze: bigger, better, four stories of brick and tile. Flagler's Continental Hotel was finally open in Atlantic Beach. The Florida East Coast Railway sped from Jacksonville to St. Augustine to Pablo Beach to Atlantic Beach.

Mayor Fletcher concluded his State of the City essay that December by writing about the struggling residents' faith in their destiny of their city, signing off with "By this sign, we will conquer." According to legend, those words were originally spoken by Constantine I in 321 B.C. It was just before the Battle of Milvian Bridge, which pitted the Roman emperor against Marcus Aurelius Valerius Maxentius. It is believed that the night before battle, while camped on the fringes of Rome, Constantine saw a vision in the sky: a fiery cross, underneath it the words *In hoc signo vinces*—"In this sign you will conquer." How appropriate that Mayor Fletcher used the words of Constantine, a battle cry inspired by a fire in the sky.

❧ 3 ❧

Kalem Comes to Town

For the motion picture industry
our venture was almost epoch-making.
—Gene Gauntier

Sure, there was competition for the human eye.

Magic was one such contender. There was Hungarian performer Ehrich Weiss. The stage name was Harry Houdini, the name on the marquee resting on the nickname below it: "The King of Cards." He drew huge audiences and not simply by having them squint at his sleight of hand. Houdini's tricks were life-threatening spectacle. The handsome Houdini, with a beret-shaped head of curls and slick eyes of a miscreant, escaped from handcuffs and chains and straitjackets while dangling from ropes or suspended in water. One audience in London watched an elephant and its trainer disappear.

Another challenger was stereoscopic photography, which brought visual fantasy home. Invented years earlier in 1838, stereoscopy placed two images of the same view side by side, each picture taken from a slightly different perspective. When viewed through a binocular apparatus, the brain is fooled into seeing a third image, a three-dimensional picture created by the first two. Stereoscopy became a novelty used in all genres of photography. Some were traditional, such as viewing natural wonders and tourist sites—

see downtown Manhattan as if standing on a bowery rooftop! Some were nontraditional and erotic—sneak a peek at naked women as if through a parlor peephole!

Vaudeville was still the reigning champion of mass entertainment. Opera and Shakespeare had their niche audiences, mostly the wealthy, but nothing cast as wide a net as vaudeville. The term, bastardized from the French phrase "voix de ville," meaning "voice of the city," came to be a catch-all for every manner of entertainment that scattered across a night's playbill: comedy, monologues, acts of strength, singing, mind tricks. A typical bill began with something innocuous and silent; acrobatics or unicyclists were common. From there, a gentleman may delve into a *King Lear* soliloquy or scatter sand or salt on the stage for a soft-shoe routine. The bill would close with a "chaser," something staid enough to run the audience from the theater so preparations could be made for the next show. Vaudeville had reached the height of its popularity in the early 1900s. Theaters were built for it; saloons and town halls were converted for it. Tents were hoisted across the Midwest for the traveling ensembles.

But nothing could excite and frighten and dominate like film. From those first flutters of Fred Ott's sneeze and the trotting horse on the Grand Café wall, a new and forever unmatched visual medium was born. It would lord over all the above-mentioned enterprises, leaving them to scrounge for table scraps. Stereoscopic photography would peter off slowly, eventually making a living as a D-list promotional conduit for Disney, the company that sells 3-D Viewmasters and miniature slide wheels with snippets of *Snow White*, *Aladdin*, and *The Incredibles*. Magic, as it was known a century ago, is kept on life support by 3,000-seat theaters in Las Vegas, and daredevils trading the hidden Queen of Clubs for life-threatening stunts—what is a new and improved way to die? Vaudeville's demise began with film and continued with the advent of television. Today, vaudeville is an archaic craft.

Film was ready for its close-up, and we would all be watching.

Fade In: New York City—Day.

Those new-fangled electric streetcars rumbled down Canal and Chambers and Broadway, past the black Model A's with white-walled tires. This was New York City, Manhattan, its legend beginning in 1626 when the Dutch bought the Island from the Lenape Indians for 60 guilders, or 24 dollars. That's 80 cents per square mile. By the beginning of the twentieth century, Manhattan was a labyrinth of brick, soot, and light. It was here that the American film boom took hold in the nickelodeons ("nickel" referring to price, *Odeon* a Greek word for performance hall). Film professor Ben Singer acknowledges this genesis: "Early exhibition in Manhattan holds special interest for film history . . . because Manhattan's nickelodeon boom so often has functioned as historical shorthand for the rise of movies in general." By 1908, there were more than 300 storefront theaters on the island. They were packed along the asphalt estuaries that fed into Broadway and Union Square and were hidden in the cobblestone nooks of the Lower East Side ghettos. The city was also the film industry's headquarters, and why not? It was the nation's financial and cultural hub.[1]

However, the film industry's earliest public venues were rather boorish. Visitors would wander into a penny arcade, slip a coin into Edison's Kinetoscope, turn the crank, and watch as many as 1,500 images flicker past to create the effect of motion pictures. Inside the peephole you could see girls dancing or boxers boxing. But the Kinetoscope had competition. There were other novelties, like the Lung Tester, where you blew into a tube and tried to lift the hats off the head of dolls. The Imperial Shocker, resembling a cross between a gumball machine and a cuckoo clock, was an "electric treatment" for rheumatism, headache, nervousness, debility, and all nervous disorders. Patrons grabbed the two metal handles and received a high-voltage dose of electricity.

When projection became standard issue, it changed everything. Film was no longer an intimate, one-on-one experience. It was an *event*, like prize fights or tent revivals, where one screening could reach hundreds at a time, all of them cooing and buzzing, the word of mouth exponential. Bootlegged equipment was purchased, mostly by vaudeville houses looking for a chaser between performances. Film as a chaser? Didn't this luminescent flicker enthrall the audiences? Not at first. Content was weak. It was mostly erudite, boring two-minute documentaries. Sure, the Lumières did it with *Workers Leaving the Lumière Factory*, but that was simply a convenient topic for an experiment. Other filmmakers must have taken their cue; one of those early films was *Feeding the Pigeons in Central Park*.

What saved the drooping medium from fad status was war. Conflict in Samoa, South Africa, and the Philippines became headline fodder for the country's news dailies, and audiences were hungry for "picturizations" of the overseas events. Military battles began filling those 150-foot spools known as "newsreels," which led to more films based on stories people read about in the newspaper.

Something was still missing. So far, film was imaginative only in its mechanics—a claw mechanism, filament bulb, and hand crank created an image that seemed like a ghost walking on the wall. What of content? Two films (and two directors) would change the approach forever.

Edwin S. Porter was a mechanic and projectionist, a portly doppelgänger for Louis Lumière. He was also the director of some 142 films. These included reenactments: *Execution of Czolgosz and the Panorama of Auburn Prison*, which re-created the electrocution of León Czolgosz, the assassin of President William McKinley. They included documentary: *After the Race: Yachts Returning to Anchorage, Mount Pelee in Eruption and Destruction of St. Pierre, Martinique*, and *Panoramic View of an Electric Tower from a Balloon.* And even adaptations: *Jack and the Beanstalk* and *Uncle Tom's Cabin.* And they included lots of original narrative, particularly action and comedy shorts produced for the Edison Manufacturing Company. Before Charlie Chaplin's tramp, there was Porter's tramp; in 1901 alone, Porter directed *The Tramp's Dream, The Tramp's Escape*, and *Pie, Tramp and the Bulldog.*

But in 1903, Porter and his writing partner crafted a story about a gang of Wild West cowboys taking a train hostage. It needed a good title, but Porter traditionally leaned toward dry toast (his 1903 action short was named *New York Harbor Police Boat Patrol Capturing Pirates*). For this new movie he went with *The Great Train Robbery.*

When audiences saw this eleven-minute western (shot in the East, in New Jersey and Delaware), it attacked their senses. Each cell was hand painted. During a dancing scene, the women's antebellum dresses swirled in blue and red and green. But the moment that captured audiences came at the end of the reel. In a medium close-up, the gang's leader, played by Justus D. Barnes, squinted like a spider—cold, detached. He lifted his pistol to his chest, in front of his spotted bandanna, and fired one into the lens. Barnes shattered the fourth wall with a hot round of lead, and viewers were shocked. *He's looking at us! He shot at us!* That five-second scene drenched the audience in film's chief export: suspended disbelief. Powered by gossip and outrage, *The Great Train Robbery* became a blockbuster. It toured the country ad infinitum. It even birthed a theme ride: Hale's Tours and Scenes of the World, the first theater chain, screened the film in a real railway car that rocked, jostled, and sounded a locomotive's whistle. The mark of any true success is a parody—two years later, in 1905, *The Little Train Robbery* was released. In this short, young bandits rob passengers on a kiddie train. Porter directed.

Four thousand miles across the Big Pond, Georges Méliès invented his own narrative phenomenon with *Le Voyage dans la lune* (A Trip to the Moon). With the help of his wife's wealthy family, Méliès purchased an Animatograph—an alternative name for the unlicensed Kinetoscope—for 1,000 francs.[2]

Méliès discovered that with film, illusions could be amplified, and at sixteen frames per second, the audience would have no shot at seeing the trap door or secret vest pocket. He pioneered several camera tricks. They include the multiple exposure: cranking the film spool back to shoot over film stock that's already been exposed (Ext. Funeral Home—Day. The man's spirit walks out of his body). There was also the matte shot. For this, half the lens is covered and the film is exposed. The stock is rewound, the other half of the lens is covered, and the blank half of the film strip is exposed (Int. John's House—Day. The man stares quizzically at his identical twin). He also pioneered the model shot, creating miniature replicas of cities or landscapes (Ext. Pompeii—Day. Mount Vesuvius erupts and scatters ash across the hillside).

Although Méliès had been making *féeries*, which loosely translates from French as "fantasy film," for nearly a decade, his international renown arrived with *Le Voyage dans la lune* in 1902. When audiences saw the film, they didn't see any pedestrian set pieces; there were no boudoirs or kitchens. There were no love interests or pistol-packed showdowns. This was something entirely new: a comic science fiction romp, a space odyssey that predated Stanley Kubrick's by three-quarters of a century.

In the version held by the Museum of Modern Art in New York, *Le Voyage* begins with a title card: "Méliès introduced the trick film. His work was widely shown and often imitated here at the beginning of the century. He himself here appears as the principal character." That character is Barbenfouilles, who opens the film by holding court over a gaggle of other scientists seated in a Gothic lecture hall. The scientists have long beards and pointed wizard caps, suggesting that the gap between science and sorcery isn't very wide. On the blackboard, Barbenfouilles draws a rocket en route to the moon. Perhaps outraged, excited, or both, the scientists go into an uproar.

Moments later, a group of scientists boards a bulbous, bullet-shaped rocket. A fuse is lit and they tear off into the atmosphere. Shifting to the rocket's point of view, we see the moon, which in Méliès' world is an anthropomorphic orb with a pocked complexion. In the film's most famous scene, the rocket crashes into the moon's eye, its skin melting and dribbling down its face like cake icing.

Le Voyage connected with audiences for several reasons. First, of course, was its visual esthetic: he used trick shots, hand-painted sets, and lavish costumes. Barbenfouilles' city is nowhere and anywhere, an anonymous metropolis 20,000 leagues into the future. It's a chiaroscuro urbanist landscape—rigid iron angles, pillars belching steam. Imagine German Expressionism rendered with the charm of a pop-up book. Instead of zero gravity and seas of tranquility, knowledge of which would be household facts in fifty years, the moon is a psychedelic landscape of toadstools, stumps, and rock outcroppings. Méliès' three-dimensional fantasyscapes, more artistic than realistic, more van Gogh than Caravaggio, have inspired countless filmmakers, including Jean Pierre Jeunot (*City of Lost Children*), Fritz Lang (*Metropolis*), and Tim Burton (*Sleepy Hollow, Edward Scissorhands*).

The Great Train Robbery and *Le Voyage* cemented film as not only an entertaining enterprise but a commercially viable one as well. At the beginning of 1907, *Variety* stated that a "conservative estimate" for the amount of nickelodeons in the United States was 2,500.[3] By July 1908, the *Oakland Tribune* put the national figure of 8,000.[4]

Any budding entrepreneur could buy a projector and draw a crowd. Even more lucrative, he could buy films and become a distributor. In 1909, the industry trade publication *Moving Picture World* noted that one successful exchange man made $20,000 a week. Money could be saved by copying and distributing films illegally, an offense that cost Méliès countless sums in licensing fees. In *One Reel a Week,* the autobiography of famed Hollywood producer Fred Balshofer, the author tells a story about an early job working for Sigmund Lubin, the filmmaker from Philadelphia who produced the reenactment of the Corbett-Fitzsimmons fight. Part of Balshofer's job was making "dupes," or duplicates. "In those days each moving picture company had its own trademark which was usually placed in some prominent place in the picture to ensure visibility," writes Balshofer. "The Méliès trademark was a star . . . and I spent a lot of time blocking out the trademark on each individual frame under a magnifying glass, using a camel's hair brush dipped in opaque." In 1906, a gentleman wandered into the Lubin shop and requested a copy of *Le Voyage*. Shortly after film began fluttering on the screen, the gentleman ordered them to shut if off. "Lubin stared at him wondering what was wrong. We found out soon enough when the prospective buyer shouted, 'You want me to buy that film?' Lubin wanted to know why not. 'I,' the man bellowed thumping his chest, 'I made that picture, I am Georges Méliès from Paris.' The man, quite naturally, was in a wild rage. . . . He could have become physically violent, but he soon stamped out of the room."[5]

While the Corbett-Fitzsimmons fight was the first film screened in Jacksonville in 1897, show business didn't start in earnest until the nickelodeons and theaters arrived a decade later. Exact figures regarding Jacksonville's nickelodeons are more difficult to come by, although photography helps place and trace some of the city's earliest theaters. There was the 20th Century Theater on the 200 block of West Bay Street. Its architecture was free of frills and downright uninviting: a bunker-like structure with a bar-covered ticket window. It was considered a lower-class venue, known locally as "The Fishhouse." Over the entrance, the sign read, "Wonderful marvels of the age in motion pictures." And over the exit: "Advanced creations in beautiful motion pictures." It was a third- and fourth-run theater. In an anonymous photo taken in 1908, the sign advertised the films *The Pirate* and *The Elopement*.

The Imperial Theater, set along Forsyth Street, was a brick Neo-Georgian structure designed by Roy A. Benjamin, who would contribute many theaters to the city. It had high arched windows and white trim; the electric sign blazed the venue's name in faux Persian font.

These two theaters are the bookends: one marked fashion, the other function. But the venue that split the difference was the Savoy. Filling the bustling street corner of East Forsyth Street and Main Street, next to the *Florida Metropolis* headquarters, the Savoy was a white structure with text wrapping its façade like a news crawl: "Continuous Performances from 10 a.m. to 5 p.m.," "5 Cent Admissions," "Motion Pictures." Promo cards and penny arcades speckled the sidewalk. Crowning the structure was a wire frame adorned with the theater's moniker and decorative Rococo swirls. Strings of lights dangled like clotheslines in every direction. The theater's arrival must have thrilled the owners of the neighboring Windle Hotel. The sign on the hotel's roof was overshadowed by the Savoy's electric distraction.

So you paid your five cents, entered the nickelodeon, and watched a film. Rarely do we get a picture of the world behind the ticket booth, behind the velvet curtain. The nickelodeon was a place of information and entertainment, but it was also a place of segregation and vice. In 1909, a *Moving Picture*

The Savoy Theater, one of the first nickelodeons in Jacksonville, was located on the bustling corner of East Forsyth Street and Main Street. *Florida Photographic Collection, Tallahassee, Florida*

World editor wrote, "During the past three or four years . . . any person of refinement looked around to see if [he or she were] likely to be recognized by anyone before entering the doors."[6]

But enter they did. And what did they see? What were Jacksonville's nickelodeons—sensoriums of sight and sound—really like? Step inside, step inside, only a nickel, and witness the wonderful marvels of the motion picture. . . .

⊰ ⊱

You might have previously known it as a cigar shop or clothier, but now it's a nickelodeon, nickel theatre, spectatorium, or whatever word they're using this week. After passing the barking carney, the monkey grinding the organ, or, as the reformers alleged, pimps trolling for young women, you would enter and wander past a few electrically lit house rules—such as "Hats Off." "No Smoking" was the most heavily enforced house rule; film was made of highly flammable nitrate.

Once inside the seating area, you could pick from one of the roughly 200 chairs. Not long like pews or welded together like a baseball stadium, but loose and unattached. If you were in one of your town's bigger venues, the "blacks only" section was upstairs to the rear.

Look around and you would see anyone and everyone: whites, blacks, Hispanics, Poles, and Jews. Wealthy arts patrons displaced by the recently incinerated Park Opera House sat near swarthy saloon regulars. What you were not likely to see was families, as many of the playbills were filled with racy material. Take for example *The Model's Ma*, produced by Biograph. "The model's mother gives instructions to the artist that her daughter may not pose unclothed. The artist pushes the mother out of the studio, and the girl poses clothed as instructed, but the artist paints her as a nude." Or *The Boy, the Bust, and the Bath*, where a young boy "sets up a plaster bust of a woman in a boardinghouse bath, fooling a whole series of would-be voyeurs."[7] In 1901, Edison released *What Demoralized the Barbershop*, the answer being a raised skirt at the top of the salon's stairway. Some blamed the French for the perverted content. *Moving Picture World* carried a particularly Francophobic take on the issue in 1908. "The foremost French makers maintain a fine standard of excellence, but they owe it to American taste to eliminate some features," the editorial read. "The frank way in which marital infidelities are carried on . . . the eating of rats and cats, the brutal handling of helpless infants, do not appeal to the American sense of humor."[8] Later that year, New York's anti-vice mayor George McClellan closed all the nickelodeons, citing "the supposedly poor moral condition of the darkened rooms and the kind of films shown in them." Public outcry ensued, and his reform efforts amounted to political suicide.[9]

To the rear of the theater, the owner–money collector–projectionist readies the film for screening. Unless he is enterprising enough to hire a young assistant, the gentleman will have to crank the machine all day long. Eileen Bowser writes, "To be good at his profession, [the projectionist] needed to have an understanding of electricity and the laws of optics, and he needed to be a mechanic, in order to repair the projection machine when it broke down. Often he was expected to go and pick up the reels for each day's show, either at the film exchange or railway station."[10]

The film watched would be accompanied by music. The quality varied from venue to venue. Some nickelodeons simply placed a needle on a phonograph record or flipped the switch on the self-playing piano, letting the ragtime follow the film's action at random. If the budget allowed, a theater owner could upgrade to the two- or three-piece band, likely a pianist and percussionist. Sometimes the musicians knew the plot points, other times not—a drumroll for a fistfight might ignite suspense, but a drumroll for a kiss would inspire giggling. The most advanced venues used full orchestras and sound effects men. The musicians practiced alongside the film to make sure the *accelerandos*, *adagios* and *crescendos* were timed appropriately. Behind the curtain, the sound effects man would be armed with an arsenal of tools: a slide whistle for a slip on a wet floor, a cowbell for a vase to the cranium, a box full of starch for footsteps in the snow.

When the house lights rose, you had either been exhilarated or offended. As you filed out with the rest of the audience, you would see one more electric sign, which is as much a message to you as it was to the industry writ large: "Stay As Long As You Like."

But for Jacksonville and Los Angeles, being a conduit was not the aim. They did not want to simply be the venue, the vessel by which imagination is transported. These were cities looking to be Ponce de León, the explorer, the boldface name in the history book. Anyone can present creativity. But to birth it, to carry it *in utero*—that's a legacy. The moving picture, "movie" in its familiar nickname, was the type of phenomenon that could define a city. And Jacksonville was looking for an identity.

As it happened, money and film came from the same place: north of the Mason-Dixon line. The North claimed most of the major production companies as well. Edison and others were set up in New Jersey and New York. There was Biograph, the New York powerhouse and competitor to Broadway (in fact, one of Biograph's earliest films was a stop-motion documentation of the wrecking of the Star Theatre on Broadway). Vitagraph was also in Manhattan. French firms Pathé, Gaumont, and Méliès set up shop there as well. Sigmund Lubin was a train stop south in Philadelphia, where he oversaw the operations of Lubin's Palace, the largest movie theater of the era, which seated some 800 spectators. Selig Polyscope, Essanay, and Kalem were farther west in Chicago.

The problem, however, was that the North provided little in the way of visual variety. Nearly every film was shot indoors. In New York, filmmakers were scattered in spaces of all shapes and sizes. Biograph worked from a brownstone at 11 East 14th Street. Edison's studio was in the Bronx. Others were on the Lower East Side, Midtown, or across the river in Fort Lee, New Jersey. Because of the weather and space limitations, many of the early films these filmmakers produced were adapted plays. Naturally, Shakespeare was an early favorite, despite the fact that they had to fit five acts into 500 feet of film. There was *Julius Caesar*, *Richard III*, *King Lear*, and *The Merry Wives of Windsor*. Some did venture outdoors: Vitagraph's *Romeo & Juliet* staged the sword fight between Tybalt and Mercutio at Central Park's famous Bethesda Fountain, its bronze-winged seraph the backdrop. Popular authors of the day were adapted as well: Hawthorne, Faust, Tolstoy, Verne, and others. Both Essanay and Edison produced holiday versions of Charles Dickens's *A Christmas Carol*.[11]

There were other problems with working in a cold environment. In *One Reel a Week*, Academy Award–winning director of photography Arthur Miller discusses one of the biggest among them. "Static . . . was produced in the camera by friction of the celluloid side of the film as it slid by the steel pressure plate at the aperture as well as the velvet at the light traps of the magazine. The blue static sparks exposed the negative causing the developed negative to be full of black marks resembling branches of a Christmas tree. . . . When the weather turned cold, static was the bugaboo of all cameramen."[12]

Gene Gauntier was one of the silent era's pioneers, and not because just anyone involved in the industry in those days was a pioneer. She was an actress and a screenwriter; she wrote more than 300 screenplays during her career, including *The Days of '61*, the first film ever made about the Civil War. She came to New York from Kansas City shortly after the turn of the twentieth century, tumbling into filmmaking with the help of Frank Marion, cofounder of Kalem Pictures. In her autobiography *Blazing the Trail*, which was serialized by *Woman's Home Companion* beginning in 1928, Gauntier concurs with Miller's assessment. "There were many forms of [static], and all of them were disheartening. One kind resembled forked lightning running from top to bottom of the picture; and again it took the form of sheet lightning, white flashes moving from side to side. . . . For years, war was waged on it, the Eastman Company joining the struggle and putting out a nonstatic film, which at first was not satisfactory."[13]

Attempts were made to write around the elements, but they proved unsuccessful. Gauntier writes, "Because of the failure of the studio picture, Mr. Marion cast about for one that could be taken to open air in winter, and *Washington at Valley Forge* was the result." Gauntier wrote the script and starred. "It was made in blizzards and the coldest weather of the year," she writes. "A military school up the Hudson cooperated and a passable picture was produced, but at the cost of . . . frostbites and sickness."[14]

Filmmaking's most necessary resource was light. The film of the era required much of it. At the time, the stock had an estimated film speed of 4. Today, a typical film speed is 400. Synthetic sun alternatives were available, such as the Cooper Hewitt's mercury vapor lamps, but they were expensive. Natural sunlight was the easy answer. But up north, gray days were aplenty. To maximize those quick slivers of winter sun, many studios worked from glass-enclosed rooftop studios.[15]

The latter months of 1908 were proving particularly severe; the short winter days left little in the way of natural sunlight. It was apparent that something, anything, needed to be done. Marion, who along with co-principals Samuel Long and George Kleine comprised the upper brass of Kalem (their initials K-L-M, when said phonetically, became the company's name), decided to send a film crew somewhere new. In her account, Gauntier writes, "In November, Mr. Marion, having decided not to risk another winter fighting northern weather conditions, went to Florida to determine the practicality of sending a stock company there to work the entire season." But where in Florida? One place stood out. A place where the railway tracks from New York ended at a grand central station. A place with forests and beaches and a river. A place in the sun.[16]

⁂

It is a cosmopolitan city.

It has a population of about 48,000.

It is located on the noble St. Johns River, which, with its tributaries, affords 1,000 miles of inland navigation.

It has a waterfront of over seven miles.

It is the gateway to Florida and the West Indies.

It has direct communication with every important city in the United States via ten railway systems.

It is the business metropolis of Florida.

It has twenty-eight wholesale groceries.[17]

This is how the Jacksonville Board of Trade synopsized the city in its 1906 report *Jacksonville and Florida Facts*. It was here, in this cosmopolitan waterfront gateway metropolis that Kalem shipped its first-string creative team, led by Sidney Olcott. A well-respected director, Olcott had been lured from Biograph a year earlier with a contract that promised $10 a picture. As part of his responsibilities for this southern venture, Olcott was charged with selecting a stock company of actors and crew. Among them were actor James Vincent, a chisel-chinned rookie, cameraman Ben Owens, and Gauntier, the ingénue with soft midwestern features. Olcott first worked with Gauntier while directing *The Days of '61*.

"We were Florida bound," Gauntier writes, "the first film company to be sent out of New York for such a lengthy stay. Our departure created a sensation within the industry."[18]

The Roseland Hotel in the Jacksonville suburb of Fairfield was chosen as Kalem's boardinghouse, headquarters, and studio (a wooden platform adjoining the Roseland was built for $400). It was a charming farmhouse with three acres of lawn, a bowling alley, tennis courts, and croquet grounds. The Roseland's proprietor, Ma Perkins, was "a stout jolly widow, who was motherly, smiling, and always ready to drop down in the rocking chair on the big front veranda for a chat." Ma Perkins was used to dealing with these eccentric passers-through; the Roseland also rented to acts booked at the Ostrich

The Roseland Hotel in the suburb of Fairfield was the boardinghouse and studio for Kalem Pictures when the troupe first arrived in Jacksonville in 1908. *Florida Photographic Collection, Tallahassee, Florida*

Farm, just up Talleyrand Avenue. "If the Webers, a family of acrobats, were not practicing their act on the lawn before the veranda," writes Gauntier, "the man with the trained goats was putting his animals through their tricks, a juggler was practicing his stunts, or the trained dogs were perfecting themselves."[19]

Because Jacksonville had a plethora of backdrops, new stories were everywhere. You could pluck them from the milieu like oranges from the neighboring orchard. To the east, Fernandina was dense with tropical thickets and jigsaw blade sawgrass—it was cast as the Amazon and other anonymous jungle wilds. There were also the sands of Manhattan Beach—lovers stranded on an island or perhaps explorers looking for the X on the treasure map. The Strawberry Creek bridge was only a few hundred yards from the Roseland, and according to Gauntier, "fierce battles were fought on it; it was burned (with smoke pots); many a chase was staged on its uneven boards, and horses jumped from it twenty feet into the water." To the southwest were dense forests, perfect for a re-creation of the Battle of Olustee, fought forty-four years earlier amid the pines of Lake City. Thanks to the city's downtown architectural variety, New England and Old Europe could be re-created within minutes.[20]

But creative inspiration was only part of the equation. In *Lights! Camera! Florida!* Richard Alan Nelson discusses why Jacksonville was an attractive center for filmmaking on several levels.

> Although mountains were lacking and the summers were sultry, other factors favored Jacksonville as a potential film center. Among them . . . relatively inexpensive labor costs when compared to the Northeast, excellent hotel and rental housing facilities, favorable rail and ocean liner freight rates (important particularly for the shipment of props and costumes), and a cosmopolitan citizenship. Jacksonville had the further advantage of being a major theatrical tour stop for both white and black actors, with thespians "between engagements" open to the enticements of movie employment at $3–4 per day or $20–25 a week.[21]

The Kalem crew quickly went to work—averaging two pictures a week—with only one order from back home: outdoor shoots only. They began writing the southern landscape into every script. "My screen work was all strenuous," writes Gauntier. "Horseback rides for hours each day, water scenes in which I committed suicide or floated on spars in shark-infested waters, climbing trees, coming down ropes from second-story windows, jumping roofs or rolling down to be caught in blankets, overturning skiffs, paddling canoes, a hundred and one 'stunts' thought out to give the action which Kalem films demanded." The film was shipped back to New York by train for developing and printing, then back to Jacksonville for editing.[22]

The first one-reeler completed was *A Florida Feud; Or, Love in the Everglades*, a story of poor whites living on the outskirts of Jacksonville. In its press materials, Kalem described the film as "a strong dramatic story in

Some of the Kalem Players, including Gene Gauntier (*first row, second from left*) and Sidney Olcott (*first row, fourth from left*), in front of the Vim Theatre in 1910. *Florida Photographic Collection, Tallahassee, Florida*

real tropical scenery" that presented a "very faithful portrayal of conditions which exist in certain portions of Florida today." It hit theaters in January 1909, and despite irking some locals for its portrayal of them, it was an immediate success. Kalem pushed the envelope even farther in its portrayal of southerners in *The Cracker's Bride*, about an adulterous wife who has an affair. Her husband violently squelches the relationship, then flees into the swamp. *Variety* panned it, liberally using the adjectives "disgusting" and "revolting."[23]

Eighteen films were produced in Kalem's first season down south. The newspapers grouped them as either the Florida series, the Sunny South series, or the Southern series. The movies included *The Octoroon, A Story of the Turpentine Forest, The New Minister; Or, the Drunkard's Daughter, The Seminole's Vengeance; Or, the Slave Catchers of Florida, The Northern Schoolmaster, The Fish Pirates; Or, the Game Warden's Test, A Poor Wife's Devotion, The Orange Grower's Daughter*, and *Sporting Days in the South*. Some of the films caught left hooks from the critics and the public, particularly *The Cracker's Bride*, but others found favor among local audiences, especially Kalem's Civil War pictures that were sympathetic to the South such as *The Old Soldier's Story* and *The Escape from Andersonville*.

The 1908 winter season, on the whole, was a moneymaking affair. William Wright, Kalem's treasurer, relayed to *Moving Picture World* that in the Florida series' first week of release, business increased by 1,000 percent. And so the following year, Kalem returned to Jacksonville. While the Roseland remained the company's humble southern headquarters, Kalem's New York studios, offices, and laboratories moved to a bigger facility. This time, the goal was twenty-three films, which continued Kalem's critical view of life in Florida: a mysterious paradise saturated in hooch, misery, and a conspiring Dixie kakistocracy. A sampling of the movie titles says it all: *A Slave to Drink, The Seminole's Trust, The Seminole Half-Breeds, The Exile Chief, The Romance of the Trained Nurse, The Egret Hunter, The Railway Mail Clerk*, and *The Fisherman's Granddaughter*.

At this point, it's important to examine why and how exactly Jacksonville became the first Hollywood. Thanks to Kalem, Jacksonville pioneered several creative and business trends in that first season that would be adopted by the larger industry shortly thereafter.

Exhibit A: Kalem established the first location "studio" in the United States. It was the first permanent filmmaking location that wasn't in the Northeast and the first to prove that a temperate climate was essential to filmmaking. Kalem predated the first permanent West Coast studio by three years. And while the Roseland House was not exactly Paramount or Universal or any of the other gated citadels, it was an ancestor with similar DNA: a singular location that housed facilities for production, editing, makeup, and costuming, with exteriors filmed in the open-air "back lot."

Exhibit B: Kalem, and thereby Jacksonville, was also the first to employ a "stock company" of talent and crew. Kalem borrowed the practice from traveling theater companies; it was later adapted into the "star system" of Louis B. Mayer, Adolph Zukor, and the Warner brothers in the 1930s and 1940s.

Exhibit C: Jacksonville helped usher in location shooting for the purposes of authentic narrative filmmaking. In New York, Manhattan greenhouses were festooned with handmade backdrops to trick our retinas into believing it was Rome or the South Pacific. Florida cured that illusion, shattering those literal and figurative glass ceilings. In 1910, the *New York Daily Mirror* asked, "How far will a modern motion picture company go to get 'atmosphere' for a film drama? This question has been answered a good many times ... during the last year or two."[24]

And so the love affair with Jacksonville began. As Gauntier put it, "For the motion picture industry [Kalem's] venture was almost epoch-making, establishing as it did new artistic standards, particularly in atmosphere, and inaugurating the custom of traveling far and wide in search of effective and authentic backgrounds."[25] In the coming years, an estimated thirty production companies set up camp in town, helping the city earn the nickname of "World's Winter Film Capital." But there was another place that could match Jacksonville vista for vista.

❧ 4 ❧

Meanwhile, on the West Coast . . .

Bust the Trust—Go Independent
—Anti-MPPC Flyer, circa 1910

There was no tinsel or glamour or stars or extras. There were no red carpets or green screens. Before any of that, it was a border-crossing sanctuary on the Pacific known as Mission Nuestra Señora Reina de los Angeles. Just pineapples and kiwis and dust and mist.

Like Florida, California dates back to the mid-sixteenth century. But its modern roots are most often traced to 1769, when the Spanish set out to establish a new religious colony. Father Juan Crespi, one of the sixty-seven men on that Spanish expedition, was searching for a place to set up Franciscan missions. When he found the spot, Crespi described it in his diary:

> After traveling about a league and a half through a pass between low hills we entered a very spacious valley, well grown with cottonwoods and alders, among which ran a beautiful river from north-northwest, and then, doubling the point of a steep hill, it went on afterward to the south. . . . As soon as we arrived, about eight heathen from a good village came to visit us; they live in this delightful place among the trees on the river.[1]

Crespi was looking at the Los Angeles River. Running along the western portion of the valley, the river picks up steam along its fifty-one miles to Long Beach thanks to tributaries from the San Gabriel and San Susanna Mountains as well as the Arroyo Seco and the Tuyunga Wash. The "eight heathen" Crespi referred to were likely from one of the local indigenous tribes, Tongva, Chumash, or Gabriellino. To purify the landscape, these Christian crusaders quickly acquired naming rights. The river's original name, the Porciúncula, refers to one of the Franciscan chapels back in Assisi. The "very spacious valley" was co-opted by Saint Fernando.

By the late eighteenth century, this riverfront settlement was known as El Pueblo de Nuestra Señora Reina de los Angeles del Rio de Porciúncula (The Town of Our Lady the Queen of the Angels on the River Porciúncula). Africans and Indians and Spaniards made up the majority of the forty-six settlers.

California was passed from the Spanish to the Mexicans and finally to the Americans in 1847. The gringos lopped off the town's polysyllabic prefix, and it became Los Angeles, which was incorporated as a city in 1850.

By the 1890s, the local economy was being supported by several products, among them flowers (hibiscus, jacaranda, and bougainvillea grew wild), fruit (the rich soil and cool temperatures were ideal for peaches, figs, strawberries, and kiwi), and oil (at one point Los Angeles supplied one-quarter of the world's petroleum). But California was a vacant lot.

Harvey Wilcox and his wife Daeida were among the first developers to arrive. The Topeka couple had made their name in real estate, and in 1883 they bought two tickets on the Atchison, Topeka and Santa Fe Railway to California. The Wilcoxes purchased three tracts of land, which they subdivided and sold. But this place wasn't strictly business for them. Harvey and Daeida found solace in the Cahuenga Valley. The vistas were a temporary narcotic to numb their pain. Their nineteen-month-old baby, the couple's only child, had recently passed away.

There was one spot in particular where the Sunday drives always seemed to take them: a fig and apricot orchard appendixed to the Cahuenga. The Wilcoxes acquired it and made it their winter home. But what to call this Xanadu? During a train trip back to Topeka, Daeida struck up a conversation with a wealthy lady who made several references to her own country home. It was named Hollywood, after a Dutch settlement in Dwolle, Netherlands. Daeida liked the name, and she gave it to their California property.

So what made this suburb a film utopia? The same reasons that made Jacksonville attractive. Together, the two cities evolved into getaways for the production companies in the Northeast and Midwest. Richard Nelson states it simply: "Both satisfied the underlying need for a warm sunny climate in which to work, with a similar newness and variety of scenic locales." Jacksonville had every visual backdrop offered in California except mountains: oceans, beaches, rivers, interesting architecture. Both had a municipal and economic infrastructure for a small business to plug into and thrive.[2]

The film industry tested other locations as well, Cuba and Arizona among them. But there was something else at play, a gathering storm, and its eye was fixed over Thomas Edison's Manhattan headquarters.

૱ ૱

One thousand and ninety three patents.

That's how many Edison received during his career. Among those are the famous—the incandescent electric lamp (patent #12631) and the phonograph (#227679)—and the not so famous—the bucket conveyer (#991433) and the "flying machine" (#970616). The list, which averages out to twenty-one patents annually during his 51-year career, reflects more than just intelligence, pragmatism, and a sharp mind. Edison was obsessively competitive. He wanted credit for his ideas and the spoils that come with credit.

As relayed in the first chapter, Edison lost ownership of the filmmaking process on August 24, 1891, when he chose to not pay the extra $150 for the Kinetoscope's foreign patent. He did not believe there was money to be made in filmmaking. Meanwhile, a gaggle of foreign filmmakers—including the Lumières—had borrowed liberally from Edison and each other as they created their own motion picture cameras.

The industry was already corrupt with regard to both product quality and business ethics. As demand grew for new films, nickelodeons went to great lengths to keep a fresh supply. Oftentimes, that meant copying or illegally obtaining films and scraping the trademark off each frame. It meant handing bribes to distributors to guarantee the best new releases. It meant shipping films to multiple theaters without sending any revenue to the producers. As a result, the film quality was oftentimes terrible—sprocket holes were torn, making the film skitter across the projector's bulb or the film was scratched, a torrential downpour of nicks and tears on every frame.

For skeptics, the film quality was external proof of the industry's internal corrosion.

For Edison, adding insult to injury was the fact that foreign film producers, the same ones that had borrowed his ideas free of charge, produced so many films seen in the American market. According to the 1909 issue of *Ciné-Journal*, a French film publication, for every forty French-made prints ordered in Europe, 150 would be ordered in the United States. And those French films didn't have a Baptist's aesthetic. Risqué content was the rule, not the exception.[3]

In an effort to control the bootlegging exchange men and camera manufacturers, enforce patents, and stabilize the industry, Edison created a guild of producers and distributors, the Motion Pictures Patents Company (MPPC), that would exist under one set of standards and rules. He enlisted them via friendship or force, whichever was necessary. His first target was Pathé, the French film and distribution company that in 1907 held the largest part of the American market. "Pathé was the one company that would have had the resources to challenge the Edison claims . . . but Pathé did not contest."[4] The company joined the MPPC.

The other major production and distribution companies followed suit: Vitagraph, Lubin, Selig, Méliès, Kalem, Essanay, and Chicago distributor George Kleine. The last to join was Biograph, a bitter professional enemy of Edison. For years the two had been engaged in a legal battle over patent infringements that featured federal court decisions, federal court appeals, negotiations, and settlements. In a major coup, Eastman Kodak agreed to provide film stock only to members of Edison's guild.

In December 1908, the MPPC officially announced its formation. But what exactly was it? Without delving into the complexities of the company, known commonly in the industry as "the Trust," the following is a list of the union's governing rules and regulations, as interpreted and paraphrased by the author:

1. The nine members of the Trust are the only companies licensed to make motion pictures in the United States.

2. The nine members of the Trust are to pool their patent claims, and no company outside the Trust may execute those patents.

3. Exhibitors are charged $2 per week for the right to use projectors or films produced by the Trust.

4. Any exhibitor found using equipment or screening films fabricated by anyone outside the Trust will be reprimanded and potentially black-listed.

5. All films are to be rented through the General Film Company, the official distributor for the Trust.[5]

Needless to say, there was an outcry in the industry. "The Trust" was a monopoly.

What is most interesting is that Edison, the self-appointed protector of patents, was himself guilty of idea infringement. Bowser writes, "He had a habit of patenting everything in sight, without having successfully invented all of the devices he claimed. Eventually he did lose suits based on some patents. But then, as now, the small businessman did not have the resources to fight endless legal battles even if he might win them in the long run."[6] In his book *The Speed of Sound: Hollywood and the Talkie Revolution*, Scott Eyman shares an example of Edison's infringement related to his work on synchronizing picture and sound. "The partial basis for Edison's efforts was an invention by the Frenchman Auguste Baron, who received a French patent in April 1896 and an American patent in 1900, for a machine very similar to what Edison would call the Kinetophone. How did Edison utilize someone else's technology and get away with it? 'He was Edison,' says Robert Gitt, film archivist at UCLA. 'He had an awful lot of clout.'"[7]

Only a few months after the Trust was announced, the backlash began. The first to make waves were William Swanson, an exchange man out of Chicago, and Carl Laemmle, the future founder of Universal Pictures, who actually joined the Trust only to desert it months later. The two chose to pay exorbitant prices to import films from outside the United States. Rogues of lesser financial means opted for other strategies, including hijacking shipments Eastman was sending overseas. Others produced newspaper advertisements that criticized the Trust's regulations. One asked, "Good Morrow: Have You Paid $2 License to Pick Your Teeth?"[8] Joseph Miles, another exchange man, parodied the Trust's propagandist language in his brochure. "LICEnsed manufacturers, LICEnsed exchanges, LICEnsed projection machines." At the top of the brochure, the heading read, "A LOUSY STATEMENT from the PATENTS COMPANY."[9]

The number of dissenters increased, organizing under Laemmle's direction. This coalition of the unwilling birthed a term that still exists today—the *independent*.

Known as "infringers" and "outlaws" to Trust loyalists, "the Independents" was the collective name for the many anti-Trust factions that had popped up everywhere: the Film Renters Protective Association and the National Independent Motion Picture Alliance, both from Chicago; the Associated Independent Film Manufacturers of New York City; and the Motion Picture Distributing and Sales Company, the Carl Laemmle–led organization that served forty-seven exchanges in twenty-seven cities. Their flyers said: "Bust the Trust: Go Independent."

The battle was waged everywhere—in courtrooms, studios, laboratories, and, of course, media outlets. Cartoons in daily newspapers were a great way to reach the masses. In an effort to win public opinion, the Trust and the independents took pot shots at each other in pencil—one depicted as the greedy monopolist, the other the desperate vulture. One sketchy, one shady. In a cartoon sponsored by Laemmle, a grotesquely obese man, "The Trust" scribbled across his bulbous belly, stands next to a Mt. Everest of coins. A line of emaciated exchange men waits to pay their dues. Conversely, a Patents Company cartoon titled "Moving 'The Junkman' Along" shows a clown-faced jockey pulling a cart filled with "junk" film. Here it is the horse, with "Picture Subjects" branded on its side, that is emaciated.

While the independent companies—they included Fox, I.M.P., Thanhouser, and Mutual—spent time fighting the cause, they also moved away from it. One of the biggest side effects of the Trust was the dispersion of filmmakers across the country in an attempt to avoid the Trust's army of spies and detectives that sniffed out contraband cameras, stock, and film. Robert Sklar describes it: "The independents camouflaged their cameras, hired bodyguards to protect their cameramen and eventually scattered to locations in Cuba, Florida, Arizona and California, where they had the advantages of year-round sunshine and distance from the Trust."[10]

In *A Million And One Nights*, Terry Ramsaye concurs with Sklar: "The pressure of the Patents Company attack on the Independents was a contributing factor to the development of motion picture geography of this period. Independent motion picture taking activities in and about New York were beset by difficulties. Cameras vanished from under the nose of the guards. Mysterious chemical accidents happened in the laboratories, resulting in the loss of costly negatives. The fight was not confined to the courts." (Ramsaye's book, written in 1926, includes a brief note in its introduction: "This is, I believe, the first endeavor to set down the whole and true story of the motion picture industry. I have been in contact with the author's researchers . . . and I am aware of an unrelenting effort to exact fact. A high degree of detailed accuracy has been attained."[11] It is signed "Thom A. Edison.")

Producer Fred Balshofer was one of those questioned by Trust attorneys, but he knew how to handle the situation. In 1910, while working in Los Angeles, he was subpoenaed by the Patents Company to testify about a camera he used with the New York Motion Picture Company. "'What makes it move? Describe it. Can you make a sketch of it, and the movement?' I shook my head. 'I don't know how to draw,' I said, and then gave them a run-around story by describing another French camera that I well remembered that was not an infringement of the Edison patents. They were well aware that I was telling them a fish story, but they had to prove it."[12]

A year earlier, Balshofer and his partners in California had formed Bison Motion Pictures. But Balshofer didn't feel Los Angeles was safe from the Trust, so the crew headed into the mountain wilderness. There they cast local leathernecks in cowboy-and-Indian pictures (titles included *Davy Crockett— In Hearts United, Young Deer's Bravery, A Romance of the Prairie*, and *The Ten of Spades, Or, the Western Raffle*). "We were the first to make moving pictures at Big Bear Valley, but I must confess that the Patents Company forced this distinction upon us," Balshofer later said.[13]

Four years after its founding, the Trust was losing its grip on the market. Hopes that this nascent industry would stay within the Patents Company's inner sanctum were fruitless. As film audiences grew, so did the need for more films, distributors, and nickelodeons. It became impossible for the Trust's limited resources to police new businesses. Growing numbers created anonymity, which created insubordination. Newly established theaters and distributors simply ignored the Trust altogether. In its first year, the Trust's share of total film production, distribution, and importation was approximately 100 percent. By 1912, it was slightly more than 50 percent. The other half of the pie belonged to the independents.[14]

"The irony of it was that the Trust did not end competition, it fostered it," writes Sklar. "It gave regulation and direction to a continually shrinking segment of the motion picture industry, while outside its narrowing circle others were developing entirely different methods of filmmaking, promotion and exhibition. It did not notably improve the quality and morality of motion pictures, but it inspired others to do so."[15]

In 1912, big business was the focus of American politics. The Democratic Party's nominee for president, Woodrow Wilson, ran to reform a Republican Congress that blindly nurtured all business interests. "The government, which was designed for the people, has got into the hands of the bosses and their employers, the special interests," wrote Wilson in his famous book *The New Freedom*. "An invisible empire has been set up above the forms of democracy."[16] Six months after Wilson was nominated, the Republican administration, working under President William Taft, began filing suit against monopolistic corporations. Among them was the Motion Picture Patents Company, which it charged with violating the 1890 Sherman Anti-Trust Act. What better way for a political party to showcase its image makeover than to investigate the image maker?

The United States Government vs. The Motion Picture Patents Company involved days and months and years of litigation—the transcripts from the court case, part of the holdings of the Museum of Modern Art Film Study Center in New York, fill six massive volumes. The Trust continued as a paper tiger for several years, but the courts finally announced its legal time of death in 1917.

While the wicked witch was dead, the Trust's centrifugal effect lingered: it helped inspire—or frighten—an industry out of New York and Chicago and into new territories. But in the wake of one monopoly's death, another was being born.

❧

Adobe buildings and ranch houses, car barns and Chinese laundries. While the Trust huffed and grumbled back east, this is where Act I of Hollywood history was being shot.

Reports of early filmmaking in Los Angeles are scant. The trail leads back to Colonel William "Bud" Selig, who sent director Francis Boggs and cameraman Thomas Pearsons west in 1907 to shoot *The Count of Monte Cristo*, the first film made in California. All of the interiors had been shot back in Chicago, but they needed breaking waves and beaches to tell the story of French sailor Edmond Dantès' search for island treasure. Never mind that none of the original actors made the trip west—the second half of the film had to be entirely recast in California (Boggs took a role; so did a homeless hypnotist). The crew set up shop temporarily in a Chinese laundry on Olive Street. Shortly thereafter, Selig established a studio in Edendale, a suburb of LA.

Following Selig's crew in 1909 was Biograph, whose cast and crew included D. W. Griffith, Mary Pickford, and Billy Bitzer, and the New York Motion Picture Company, the first independent to venture west. Biograph chose a vacant car barn on the corner of George and Pico Streets. Balshofer was among the New York Motion Picture Company crew that arrived in Los Angeles on Thanksgiving that year.[17]

"We were among the first of the moving picture companies to begin building a moving picture center in California," wrote Balshofer. "Los Angeles at that time was a sprawling city of approximately 250,000 residents, many of whom were Spanish-speaking. Their customs and gentle way of life immediately won my admiration and friendship."[18]

But the distinction of being the first studio in Hollywood proper goes to David Horsley's Nestor Company, originally the Centaur Film Company. The future film mogul grew up in Durham, England, and at age 10 lost his arm from the elbow down after being hit by a passing locomotive. The family moved to Bayonne, New Jersey, in 1884.

His first professional endeavor was a pool parlor on Bayonne's Avenue D. Among his regular clientele was Charles Gorman, an unemployed scenic artist for Biograph. After Horsley's pool parlor went out of business, the two decided to start a film company. For the operation's name, they combined half of Gorman's name—the man—and half of Horsley's name—the horse—and called themselves Centaur, after the mythical equine creature.

Their Bayonne headquarters were on 900 Broadway. The quiet storefront, two plate-glass shop windows with "Centaur Film Co." stenciled on them, could have been a laundry or a china shop. But behind the building was a lot measuring 100 feet long by 25 feet wide. Gorman and Horsley split the work of getting the lot prepped for filmmaking. Gorman, familiar with scene construction, built a large wooden platform and hung wires draped with muslin to diffuse the sunlight. Horsley built a camera using a jackknife, a screwdriver, film projector sprockets, and a wooden box. Their first film, a one-reel drama, was *The Cowboy's Escape.*

But even little Centaur didn't escape harassment by the Trust. Horsley did attempt to join the cabal, going through the proper measures by filling out an application in 1908, but was denied. Three Trust representatives visited Centaur's small shop, eyeing it with disdain. "This son of a sea cook ain't got nothing," one Trust representative said. "We won't give him a license and he won't last thirty days." Centaur became an independent by default.[19]

As the Trust contracted in size, the outsiders suffered. The General Film Company cut off its supply to anyone who didn't have a license. Horsley, however, was still making pictures—he employed a burly man armed with an ax handle to stay within six feet of his camera in case spies came looking for patent infringement. Every week Centaur produced a western, a drama, and a Mutt and Jeff comedy, a live-action version of the famous comic strip that originated in William Randolph Hearst's *San Francisco Chronicle*. Centaur sold 120 prints per week. Word spread that fresh reels could be found with the one-armed man in Bayonne.[20]

By 1911, the Trust and the weather had cramped Centaur—only so many cowboys can rustle in dirty snowdrifts. Horsley was partial to Florida, but his chief director Al Christie was pulling for California. According to lore, they flipped a coin for it and California landed heads up. So that October, Horsley, Christie, and their minions loaded their equipment and costumes on a train and headed to California. Perhaps by coincidence, 1911 is the same year the trade publication *Moving Picture World* established its first West Coast correspondent.

Hollywood's first studio was the old Blondeau Saloon, a watering hole on the corner of Sunset Boulevard and Gower Street. Just as he had in Bayonne, Gorman built a wooden platform and hung muslin to cut the sun. Horsley renamed the company the Nestor Company. Actors hit their marks in the yard, negatives were developed on the screen porch of the Blondeau, and printing took place at the laboratory back in New Jersey. Business was so good that Nestor caught the eye of Laemmle's Universal Film Company, which had begun systematically consuming all of the independent companies operating out west. On May 12, 1912, Universal bought Nestor; Horsley got $175,000 in preferred stock ($3.6 million in 2006 dollars) and $204,000 in common stock ($4.2 million in 2006 dollars) and was elected treasurer of Universal, which earned him a salary of

$10,400 a year ($218,000 in 2006 dollars). A year later, as power struggles were increasing inside the company, Horsley sold his interest in Universal to Laemmle. He would not accept a check, so the balance of monies owed was brought in the back of a car, tied in bundles of one-, two-, five-, ten-, and twenty-dollar bills.[21]

Horsley's next film enterprise arrived via Noah's ark in 1915. After a heavy sales pitch from a salesman known as Mr. Tudor, Horsley bought the troubled Bostock Animal and Jungle Show. The fifty-eight lions and two elephants and countless tigers, leopards, bears, and kangaroos were shipped from London to Brooklyn, then loaded on freight cars and sent to Los Angeles. He leased a 300-by-350-foot space on Washington and Main, spending $47,500 on grandstands, cages, and 20-foot-high concrete fences.[22]

When the public failed to show up, Horsley shifted back to film to create animal pictures. His crew built a concrete platform in the center of the arena for the camera. It was surrounded by a moat to protect the cameraman. Backdrops were painted for every natural habitat: savannah grass and baobab trees for the African lions and elephants, Rocky Mountain ledges for the bears and pumas.

The crew produced several five-reel animal pictures: *Too Much Elephant*, *The Leopard's Bride*, and the Stanley in Africa series. But they weren't successful enough to save the expensive enterprise. In 1915 Horsley had more than $400,000 saved. By 1919, Horsley's ark had eaten through all of that and more, leaving him $38,000 in debt. His final movie was *Sin* in 1926.

David Horsley passed away in 1933 and is interred at the Hollywood Forever Cemetery on Santa Monica Boulevard, the sprawling graveyard where townhouse-sized mausoleums are shaded by model-thin palm trees. (True to its Tinseltown roots, the cemetery is equipped for live webcasts of its funeral services.) Horsley rests alongside Hollywood pioneers Fred Balshofer and Harvey Wilcox.

Horsley is joined at Hollywood Forever by many who followed the trail he blazed, those who helped establish the film town as *the* film town: Cecil B. DeMille, the legendary director who shot Hollywood's first feature-length film, *The Squaw Man*; William Beaudine, director for Goldwyn, Metro, and Warner Brothers; and Douglas Fairbanks, the actor mentored by D. W. Griffith and married to Mary Pickford. It was Fairbanks, along with Griffith, Pickford and Charlie Chaplin, who formed United Artists in 1919.

Many of the previously mentioned companies—Fox, Paramount, Warner Brothers, and Metro-Goldwyn-Mayer—still populate Hollywood. But some of those same names were in Jacksonville too. Films were attaching themselves to both cities. Audiences were greeted with title cards that read "Made in Jacksonville, Florida" or "A Hollywood Film." One city proclaimed itself "the World's Winter Film Capital," the other "the City of Angels." Maybe the hint was already there as to which would be the blessed one.

⇥ 5 ⇤

A Film Town Is Born

Hear me boys, we'll sure turn out a few films around this man's burg.
—Elmer Walters, Motograph

It was 1911, and Jacksonville was no longer an adolescent, bog-front boon-docks sitting at the foot of century-old live oaks. In the three short years after Kalem arrived, Jacksonville had grown up in nearly every way.

It had grown in population—according to the U.S. census, Jacksonville was by far the largest city in Florida with its 57,699 residents. The next largest was Tampa (37,782). Miami and Orlando were still in the low four digits (5,471 and 3,894 respectively).[1] Inevitably, the growth spread into the city's suburbs. Murray Hill and Lackawanna became neighborhoods for railroad employ-ees. Blacks migrated to Highland Heights and College Park. Springfield expanded north, pushing toward the Trout River. Houses filled the empty spaces off Talleyrand Avenue near the Roseland Hotel. Linking them all were the Jacksonville Electric Company's wires, which hung as low as clotheslines. According to the Jacksonville Chamber of Commerce, city real estate values more than quadrupled from 1900 to 1914 (from $11 million to $50 million), a growth matched by the increase in personal property values (from $2 million to $9 million).[2]

The city had grown up—literally. Once quaint and stocky, the city's new buildings competed with each other, creating a class of highbrow, fantasy sky-scrapers to rival those in New York, Chicago, Boston, even St. Louis. The Ma-sonic Temple, a wide-brimmed homage to the Midwest fashioned by archi-tecture firm Mark & Sheftall, could have emanated from the imagination of Louis Sullivan, the Chicago architect known as "the father of the skyscraper." Built in 1912, the Masonic Temple was five stories of reinforced concrete and brick, each floor capped by an eyebrow of cryptic freemason symbols that wrap the building like a hieroglyphic stock ticker. Other new high-rises and hotels of ten, twelve, even sixteen stories rose with head-scratching frequency. On March 3, 1910, the *Florida Metropolis*, having worn through its last stitch of editorial hyperbole thanks to the relentless debut of bigger and bolder buildings, announced downtown's latest structure with quotidian indiffer-ence: "Another Ten-Story Hotel."[3]

Naturally, one of the biggest contributors to Jacksonville's metropolitan makeover was Henry Klutho, who had helped lead the city's reconstruction after the Great Fire. Two of his most popular structures, built and completed in 1911 and 1912, were the St. James Building and the Florida Life Building. In February 1910, Jacob and Marcus Cohen, owners of Wisconsin's success-ful Cohen Brothers' Department Store, bought a huge parcel on West Duval Street, the former site of the St. James Hotel, a casualty of the Great Fire. The brothers commissioned Klutho to create a new department store. The architect suggested a four-story monolith spanning an entire city block (he designed a more conservative two-story building as a backup). Two years later, in 1912, the ribbon-cutting for Cohen Brothers' Department Store, still known commonly as the St. James Building, was attended by 28,000 onlook-ers. The store was the largest building in Jacksonville and the ninth-largest department store in the United States. With its slivers of windows, webbed-glass skylight, and figurative sculptures that acted as corner supports, it was, and is, considered Jacksonville's iconic building and Klutho's definitive Prai-rie School masterpiece.[4]

Only a month after construction began on the St. James Building, Klutho began work on the Florida Life Building, the eleven-story reinforced-con-crete high-rise on North Laura Street. The slender concrete tower dwarfed the buildings it neighbored, appearing like a world atlas stuck between two James Joyce novels on a bookshelf. Underscoring the speed of progress, the

Florida Life Building owned the title of Jacksonville's tallest structure for less than a year.[5]

While easy access to lumber, a good seaport, stable financial institutions, and the ever-reliable railways fed this growth, film was and would become the city's most public and magnetic industry. In 1911 and 1912, American film producers doubled their output.[6] According to the film publication *Motography*, 5,451 films were released by American production companies in 1913.[7] (By comparison, 587 films were released theatrically in the United States in 2005.) Almost every film in 1913 was a one-reel short of roughly ten minutes. The feature-length film was still several years away from being the common format.

Jacksonville's film industry was burgeoning. The increase in local audiences was a by-product not just of metropolitan expansion but also of legal and social circumstances. For example, before the Eighteenth Amendment was passed in December 1917, prohibition was enforced on a state-to-state basis. The majority of the dry cities and counties were in the South. When Jacksonville went dry, many of the saloons became makeshift theaters. The barflies, left with a social void, spent their nickels on Chaplin, not Chivas.

Movies were increasingly attractive investment opportunities. In 1912, the total investment in the film industry was approximately $200 million (that's $4.16 billion in 2006 dollars).[8] Some of those millions could be traced to Jacksonville. In 1911, the Montgomery Amusement Company, owner of the popular Grand Theater, sent out a prospectus offering $100 shares of its motion picture theatre company. "Since coming to Jacksonville I have been told by many that my motion picture theater excels," owner Frank Montgomery wrote. The last page of the brochure is a fill-in-the-blank stock certificate, a tear-off sheet resembling a magazine subscription card. "I hereby subscribe for all or any part of _____ shares of the capital stock of the MONTGOMERY AMUSEMENT COMPANY." It would have proved a solid investment. The Montgomery Amusement Company, run by Frank Montgomery, "the Motion Picture Man," was still in business half a century later.[9]

But of course, the crux of the local industry was the studios themselves— more than thirty film production companies set up shop in Jacksonville during its heyday. It was a mishmash of major and independent companies.

Kalem, an original member of the Motion Picture Patents Company, was the first to arrive, followed by other Trust members Biograph, Lubin, and Vitagraph. As the Trust's grip on the industry weakened and the independents' defiance became more brazen, a slew of "unauthorized" film companies set up shop, among them Thanhouser, Gaumont, New York Motion Picture Company, and Motoscope. As Richard Alan Nelson writes, "the lure of fantastic profits (one could turn an uninflated $200 investment into $2,000 in less than a week) also led dozens of new firms to brave harassment and physical intimidation from the Trust and enter the marketplace."[10] And the film studio became something of a tourist attraction. Tourists could be found peeking over fences or ogling from the fringe of the set. It was the perfect pastime: the Farmer's Almanac assigned Jacksonville 272 days of sunny weather a year, and the studios, largely devoid of artificial lighting systems, worked until sunset. Add it all together and Jacksonville, at least for a time, bested Los Angeles in film production. As Ramsaye describes it in *A Million and One Nights*, "Jacksonville continued for some years to overshadow Los Angeles as the winter studio capital."[11]

Kalem, the pioneer of this whole thing, wasn't even in town in 1911. Kalem had headed overseas to find other locales. In June of that year, the Kalem crew boarded the White Star Line's *Baltic* and headed to Ireland for the second time in two years. The year before, Kalem players had traveled to Ireland to shoot *A Lad from Old Ireland*. Location shoots had come to pay off for Olcott and Gauntier and company, and the "O'Kalems," as the troupe members were dubbed in print, were diligent in capturing that authentic *Erin go bragh*. The film features peat diggers in the hills and shots of actual Irish immigrants arriving in America. The press was smitten with *A Lad from Old Ireland*, much as they had been with the Sunny South series. "The picture is genuine Irish and needs no labeling to prove it," read the *New York Daily Mirror*'s review. "It carries its authenticity on its face."[12]

At the end of its second trip to Ireland, Kalem left the Emerald Isle and kept sailing east with its sights set on the Middle East. The goal: to shoot *From the Manger to the Cross*, originally titled *The Life of Christ*. For a full year the crew stayed in the Holy Land to shoot the first American feature-length film, released in 1913. Gauntier wrote the script and played the Virgin Mary; Olcott directed and cast himself as the blind man healed by Jesus. However, the suits up north had a general distaste for features: they said they were expensive and too ambitious. More important, they said that the audience didn't have the attention span for three- and five-reelers. Olcott and Gauntier disagreed. They started a new film company in 1913. Upon its return from Palestine, Kalem didn't skipped a beat. In 1914 the company had outgrown the Roseland Hotel and begun construction on a new permanent facility in Fairfield, a "glass-roofed studio with a $20,000 lighting system and 54-by-40-foot interior stage."[13]

The first of the independents to arrive in Jacksonville was Motograph, which specialized in the smoke-and-mirrors PR bluster that has since become a Hollywood trademark. The Baltimore-based company came to Jacksonville in 1910, renting space at Dixieland Park along the St. Johns. Elmer Walters was Motograph's mouthpiece, an orator who drew on equal parts Pentecostalism and ragtime. "This is the ideal spot for us. No use going any further," Waters said. "Hear me boys, we'll sure turn out a few films around this man's burg that will create a sensation with the 'pictur' men of this blooming hemisphere."[14] For reasons that aren't quite clear—there were rumors that Trust enforcers leaned on Motograph extra hard—Motograph never made a single picture during its first and only winter and spring on the St. Johns.

Shortly after Motograph vacated the amusement park, Selig Polyscope moved in. Venturing into this frontier was nothing new for the William Selig–led studio; it was accustomed to the buckshot scatter of its crews. Selig had already dipped his toes in the Pacific with the 1908 California feature *The Count of Monte Cristo* and had dispatched cameras to other locales that included New Orleans and the Midwest. Jacksonville was perfect for Selig's new focus: animal pictures.

This genre kicked off with Selig's 1908 film *Hunting Big Game in Africa*. At the time, the media was following former president Theodore Roosevelt's safari trip through Africa. Selig, using news-daily reports as a script, shot a faux documentary starring a burly, bespectacled Teddy doppelgänger and some rented circus animals. Advertised with posters that didn't necessarily emphasize the line between fact and fiction, the film was huge at the box office. Adding to the success, *Hunting Big Game in Africa*, shot in the jungle recesses of Illinois, arrived in theaters before the actual documentary of Roosevelt's safari trip.[15]

Selig spent that financial windfall on more animal pictures. He knew that with the right lens and the right angle, Jacksonville could double for Africa. The remaining elements of authenticity—the animals—were imported. And we're not just talking lions, tigers, and bare essentials. The company brought more than 160 trained animals, including elephants, camels, and horses. Selig also had fifteen Native Americans sent east from his West Coast operation. They were cast in Seminole pictures, including *Witch of the Everglades*.[16]

Animal pictures were Dixieland Park's biggest successes starting in 1911; among the first batch were *Back to the Primitive* and *The Survival of the Fittest*. The creatures shared the screen with co-star Kathlyn Williams, an ingénue from Butte, Montana, with a head of fairly-tale curls. Williams began her career in action pictures; she starred in the first Hollywood cliffhanger, *The Adventures of Kathlyn*. After a short stint with D. W. Griffith at Biograph, she became "the Selig Girl," typecast as an animal trainer for the animal pictures that kept the company fiscally solvent. Audiences were led to believe that Williams was an actual animal trainer, but that suspension of disbelief didn't save her from reality. While shooting *Lost in the Jungle*, one of her last pictures for Selig, Williams was mauled by a leopard.

The Dixieland Park location seemed to have a revolving door. Following Selig's departure in 1912, one studio after the other after the other set up shop there. Essanay was one such tenant. George Spoor and Broncho Billy Anderson, star of Porter's *The Great Train Robbery* (he actually played three roles in the film), formed the company in Chicago; the name was a phonetic marriage of their initials, S and A. Their short stint in Jacksonville resulted in a few of the "Broncho Billy" westerns Essanay became known for.[17] Another was Vitagraph, the most prolific of America's production companies (in 1913, it produced 401 films with approximately 390,900 feet of film). Vitagraph employed Dixieland's exteriors for 1916's *The Ordeal of Elizabeth*.[18] Most ironic, Edison—the Trustmaster himself—also came to Jacksonville, the Promised Land for wayward independents and outlaws. Edison's lensmen moved into Dixieland Park during the winter of 1913/1914 but stayed for only a few months.[19] The inventor knew well the benefits of the Florida atmosphere. He had a winter home in Fort Myers from 1886 until his death in 1931. The New England–style country house with trellises, gardens, and laboratories neighbors the former estate of his longtime friend, Henry Ford.

If you took the ferry from Dixieland Park back to the mainland and headed to the 500 block of Riverside Avenue, you'd find Sigmund Lubin's cast and crew set up in the old Florida Yacht Club, another revolving-door locale (Lubin and company moved into the Yacht Club in late 1912). In November 1907, the club had moved to a new location near the mouth of Willow Branch Creek, abandoning its old structure. Lubin used it as a temporary headquarters while his Philadelphia studio and headquarters were under construction.

Lubin discovered Jacksonville en route to the Bahamas. He was so impressed that the town was written into the movie *A Honeymoon through Snow to Sunshine*, about a newlywed couple hop-scotching from chilly Philadelphia to resorts in Jacksonville, St. Augustine, Palm Beach, and Miami. When Lubin left Dixieland Park in 1912, Vim Comedy Company inherited the space.

On Eighth Street, before it crosses Talleyrand Avenue and dead-ends into the river, you'll find the spot where independent Thanhouser built its studio in 1915. Lured from Los Angeles by city officials and the Chamber of Commerce, which promised an easy and worthwhile relocation, Edwin Thanhouser came to Jacksonville, announcing in October 1915 that "his Southern branch would invest $30,000 in constructing an elaborate glass and steel facility with a daily payroll of $1,000."[20]

The studio, located at 3537 East Eighth Street, had an open-air stage large enough to accommodate eight sets. It employed 100 people in its costume department, workshops, and front offices. "The Thanhouser company . . . was described as the finest studio in the South," reported the *Florida Times-Union*. "W. Ray Johnston, in charge of finance . . . said his company was pleased with the conditions here, stating that 'light here is better and we have more clear, clean cut days than on the West Coast.'"[21]

Where Selig had Kathlyn Williams, Thanhouser had Valda Valkyrien. Known as "the movie queen of Denmark" (although she was born in Reykjavik, Iceland), Valkyrien was the star of *The Cruise of Fate, The Hidden Valley,* and *The Unwelcome Mother*. By the last picture of her career in 1919, her severe European look had morphed from sexy to stereotype, earning her a supporting role in the socialist propaganda feature *Bolshevism on Trial*. The story tells of a young soldier who believes communism offers a better way of life than democracy. To test the hypothesis, the young man's father buys an island off the coast of Florida, where the boy establishes a commune.

The studios noted above are only a few of those that shot, directed, and dramatized from the "World's Winter Film Capital." Film history's roots cannot be covered without a trip through Jacksonville. It was here that Artcraft Picture Corporation shot its first picture, *Broadway Jones*, starring actor, singer, playwright, and composer George Cohan. Artcraft was created by Adolph Zukor. The Hungarian-born mogul also founded Famous Players, later Paramount Studios. The Eagle Film Company built a studio across several acres in the suburb of Arlington. The site, which aimed to re-create Universal City in California, included both indoor and outdoor stages and a film-processing lab. William Fox, for whom the Fox Broadcasting Company and 20th Century Fox Film Corporation was named, had his first hit with *A Fool There Was*, shot in nearby St. Augustine. The film made raven-haired Theda Bara a huge star and film's first femme fatale. Bara was also party to Florida's first celebrity publicity event. While in town shooting *A Fool There Was*, politicos and photographers gathered as she planted a palm tree in the Ancient City's Plaza de la Constitución. Metro Pictures Corporation, formed in 1915, shot several pictures in Florida after a fire displaced it from New York. Founded by Richard Rowland and Louis B. Mayer, Metro later merged with the Loews theater chain and Goldwyn Picture Corporation to become Metro-Goldwyn-Mayer.[22]

But we must remember that film, by its very nature, is a history of faces: a chronology of looks, smiles, frowns, winces, furrows, and winks. And Jacksonville birthed one of the most famous faces in movie history.

≈‱

When you visited the Electric Theatre in Milledgeville, Georgia, there was no way to know that the rotund gentleman taking tickets was an accomplished vaudeville singer and performer. To them he was just theater manager Norvell Hardy. The round-bellied twenty-year-old had talent that had been road-tested with a traveling minstrel show. He used his three years at the theater to educate himself. While the audience zoned out, Hardy examined the stars on the screen: their expressions and tics, what went over, what didn't. In 1913, he got a hint about where he could become something else to the audience. Hardy's biographer John McCabe tells the story: "A Milledgeville friend who had been vacationing in Florida returned with stories of a growing filmmaking colony in Jacksonville. Since this was only two hundred miles away, Norvell decided to visit."[23]

Upgrading his marquee moniker to "The Ton of Jollity," Hardy quickly found work in this up-and-coming cultural town: singing cabaret at Cutie Pearce's roadhouse, performing vaudeville at the Orpheum Theater. For his work, he was paid $40 a week. The Orpheum also provided romance. It was there he met Madelyn Saloshin, a fellow Georgian who played in the Orpheum's pit orchestra. They were married that same year.

After the nuptials, Hardy found work mostly at night. That left time to visit the film studios during daylight hours. He often found himself in Riverside at the Florida Yacht Club, where crowds of tourists tended to gather. He was quickly upgraded from onlooker to water boy (he volunteered for free) to supporting character. In 1914, as paranoia swelled over troubling news from Sarajevo, Lubin was shooting the silly escapist comedy *Outwitting Daddy*. One of the film's characters, Reggie, was written as a fat boy who dresses up as "a bad man" to scare his brother's future father-in-law. Lubin may have never produced a better sight gag: a six-foot-two, 300-pound farceur in fake moustache and sombrero. He nailed the part (he is credited as "O. N. Hardy"), earning himself a contract that paid $5 a day.

Hardy's easy manner and portly grace endeared him to his movie mates. Actor Bert Tracey, who acted alongside Hardy, was especially kind in his nostalgia. "At Lubin [Hardy] was everywhere regarded as the life of the party, and a terrific tease and gagster. He became very popular with the Jacksonville citizens."[24] In an unwelcome return of affection, Hardy's cohorts gave him the nickname *Babe*. The Lubin studio was close to a barbershop run by an Italian named Enzo. As McCabe puts it, Enzo "loved almost everyone of the male persuasion, but took a particular fancy to Hardy. After shaving and talcing the hulking youth's face, Enzo would pat Hardy's cheeks, repeating 'Nice-a bab-ee! Nice-a bab-ee!'" The nickname *Baby* stuck, much to Hardy's chagrin. It was eventually shortened to *Babe*. Now credited as Babe Hardy, the actor was tossed into myriad roles: Fred the Simp in *The Soubrette and the Simp*, Fattie in *The Honor of the Force*, Cutie in *She Was the Other*, Percival Pilkins in *The Daddy of Them All*, along with countless traffic cops, bartenders, bellhops, and grocery boys.

But in 1915, Lubin left town, selling its assets to Vitagraph. Hardy headed to New York in search of work and found bits and pieces with many of the studios that had satellite locations in Jacksonville, Gaumont and Edison among them. But New York's steely chill was the polar opposite of Florida. Hardy returned to Jacksonville in 1915, only to find that Vim Comedy

Company had taken over the lease at the Florida Yacht Club. Vim was established by Bob Burstein and Mark Dintenfass, the man who introduced moviemaking to Hollywood legend Lewis J. Selznick. Burstein took over Florida operations in 1914 and began cranking out buddy comedies including *Pokes and Jabbs*, starring Hardy (Pokes) and his old Lubin compatriot Bobby Burns (Jabbs). Burns had sold Burstein on casting his friend Babe as Pokes. After seeing Hardy perform at Cutie Pearce's roadhouse, watching the tenor glide like a man half his size, Burstein asked him to join the Vim players.

Like an inadvertent practice run for the role that made him famous the world over, Hardy was cast in a one-reel buddy comedy about a skinny guy and a fat guy, bumbling through any number of obstacles, pratfalls, misunderstandings, obfuscations, and confrontations. It was called *Plump and Runt*, with Hardy as guess which one and the acrobatic Bill Ruge, a former circus performer and aerialist, as Runt. The duo made thirty-seven films in 1916 alone, starting with *A Special Delivery* and ending with *A Maid to Order*. Not long after *A Maid to Order* was in the can, Vim was taken over by Amber Star Film Company around 1917. Operations were moved to Dixieland Park. Hardy moved on to Los Angeles, where he met Arthur Stanley Jefferson, also known as Stanley Laurel, and film history's most enduring comedic duo was born.

Hardy wasn't the only Hollywood headliner spotted in Jacksonville. Lionel Barrymore was in town in 1914 to film *Classmates*, based on the popular Broadway play. His sister Ethel Barrymore, Broadway ingénue and early film star, was also seen in Jacksonville, her name scribbled in the guest register at the Atlantic Hotel. Mary Pickford, the biggest draw in early cinema (and she was well compensated for it: she earned a weekly salary of $2,000 a week), was often spotted with D. W. Griffith. She was the director's muse while working for Biograph. However there is no proof, visual or otherwise, that she made a film in Florida.

Hardy left Vim (and Jacksonville) with Burstein and Dintenfass at each other's necks. Lawsuits and countersuits followed, as did King Bee Film Company, the Burstein-led troupe that rose from the funeral pyre. The company specialized in cinematic plagiarism. King Bee produced Billy West comedies, cheap imitations of Charlie Chaplin's work. After all, imitation is the sincerest form of success.

⊰§ ⧫

According to the research of John B. Reitzhammer, former head of the
Florida Film and Television Commission, approximately 330 films were produced in Jacksonville from 1909 to 1917. The most common words found
among Reitzhammer's list of Florida film titles are "Confederate," "daughter,"
"Dixie," "Florida," "prison," "soldier," "smuggler," "slave," "witch," and any

An undated still from a prison-break film produced by Gaumont Pictures. *Florida Photographic Collection, Tallahassee, Florida*

number of references to alcohol (including "booze," "drink," and "drunk-ard").[25]

But the local product wasn't all civil war and slavery, intoxication and in-carceration. While those made for titillating content, Jacksonville fostered the advancement of film both artistically and technically. The most shining example, and perhaps the most overlooked, is *The Gulf Between*, produced in 1917. What made it so special? *The Gulf Between* was the Land of Oz and everything else was Kansas.

Achieving Technicolor required a prism-beam splitter behind the lens that exposed two adjacent frames of black and white film simultaneously. One was shot through a green filter, the other through a red filter. The two reels were projected simultaneously in the movie theater, one on top of the other, and the result was a dull rendition of color filmmaking. The process was pioneered by Dr. Herbert Kalmus, head of the Technicolor Corporation and former physics and electrochemistry professor. (The Society of Motion Picture and Television Engineers still gives out the Herbert T. Kalmus Gold Medal Award each year to recognize outstanding contributions in the development of color films, processing, and technique.)

Technicolor is the reason Mickey Mouse's red shorts were red in Disney's 1932 "Silly Symphonies" cartoon *Flowers and Trees*. It's the trademarked word burned onto that famous introduction for Warner Brother's *Looney Tunes*. And it's how Dorothy left her black-and-white Kansas in 1939 for the chromatic Land of Oz in *The Wizard of Oz*.

As one could imagine, Technicolor required even more light than traditional filmmaking. (Temperatures on the set of *The Wizard of Oz* bested 100 degrees because of the blazing Kliegs.) So when it came time to film the first Technicolor feature, Kalmus and company, based in Massachusetts, headed to sunny Florida in its headquarters: a fully equipped Pullman railway car.

In "Technicolor Adventures in Cinemaland," a 1938 article for the *Journal of the Society of Motion Picture Engineers*, Kalmus describes this unique mobile film depot that went south on the Florida East Coast Railway:

> The earliest Technicolor laboratory was built within a railway car. This car was completely equipped with a photochemical laboratory, darkrooms, fireproof safes, power plant, offices, and all the machinery and apparatus necessary for continuously carrying on . . . our work . . . on a

small commercial scale. . . . In 1917, the car was rolled over the railway tracks from Boston, Massachusetts, where it was equipped, to Jacksonville, Florida, where the first Technicolor adventure in feature motion picture filmmaking was to take place.[26]

The script chosen for this Technicolor feature was by Anthony Parker Kelly and J. Parker Read, Jr. *The Gulf Between* tells the story of an abandoned girl taken under the wing of an old sea captain. A few scenes later she is a young woman, and she soon falls for a handsome society fellow. However, his wealthy parents do not approve of such a lowly companion. In a twist of comeuppance, it's discovered that the young woman is actually the long-lost daughter of a fashionable, wealthy couple. All is well. Roll credits.[27]

While the story was largely ignored, the film's burst of color was undeniable—Jacksonville's land and sea were ignited onscreen, illuminating a range

The railroad car laboratory, shipped from Boston to Jacksonville, used to produce *The Gulf Between*, the first Technicolor film ever made. *Florida Photographic Collection, Tallahassee, Florida*

of colors from Tallahassee pine green to Key West sunset. But Technicolor's cumbersome means of projection (the camera required two apertures, two lenses, and two filters) was a serious obstacle, and it hampered wide distribution. Kalmus shares this in his 1938 article:

> During one terrible night in Buffalo, I decided that such special attachments on the projector required an operator who was a cross between a college professor and acrobat, a phrase which I have since heard repeated many times. Technicolor then and there abandoned . . . special attachments on the projector.[28]

Unlike the blockbusters that would follow, *The Gulf Between* is a forgotten moment. There is no record of its existence in the Library of Congress, and it is believed that only a few frames of the original have survived.

⁂

In its early incarnation, the movie theater was something shady, a den of iniquity with a five-cent cover charge. Things had changed by the mid-1910s. Not only were theaters improving their image, their numbers were growing. The Prince Theater, later renamed the Rialto, was in the Mutual Life Building, where you could see *The Perils of Pauline* and *The Exploits of Elaine*. The Arcade Theater on the corner of West Adams and Forsyth Street opened in 1915 and was proclaimed by its owner to be the largest and best-equipped movie house in the South. The Arcade's Art Deco façade was embossed with the shapes of seashells and daisies. Inside were 1,250 seats, six ceiling fans eight feet in diameter, a balcony and ladies' parlor, and a children's section "to appeal to mothers who may wish to send their children to the theatre in the care of a maid." The city also had the Strand Theater, part of Mark Strand's chain of movie houses outfitted with the glamorous pomp of a Broadway theater. Forsyth Street, the city's aorta, had become something of a Great White Way thanks to the Savoy, the Imperial, the Empress, and the Arcade and later the Republic, the Palace, the St. Johns, and the Florida Theater, which opened in 1927 and is the only venue on the strip still in business.

On the corner of Main and Duval was the Orpheum Theater, a former vaudeville house with an open roof known as "the airdome." A photo of Montgomery's Grand Theater from 1915 shows a crowd of polished shoes, black suits, and Model A's parked along the street. A trolley-sized sign for *Tillie's Punctuated Romance* starring Charlie Chaplin and Mabel Normand hangs low enough to knick the gentlemen's hats. The Grand also drew crowds with popularity contests. In a letter sent to the *Jacksonville Journal* in 1971, a reader recalls the basics of the competition. "Each book of [movie] tickets purchased carried a certain number of votes. Young men bought more books that they could use to vote for their favorite girls. . . . The prize was an automobile."[29]

One of the most sophisticated movie houses in Jacksonville was the Duval Theater, located on West Bay Street just a quick stroll from the Hotel Mason and the Florida Life Insurance Co. building. The Duval originally opened as a minstrel show venue but evolved to become a see-and-be-seen social destination (Sarah Bernhardt and Woodrow Wilson were among its patrons). The Duval's programs underscore its high society approach. On one particular evening, patrons found a fashion column reviewing what women were to be wearing that season ("poplins in new weaves, beautiful velours, serges, whipcords, crepe de chine, moirés and charmeuse are all being shown . . . tailored suits in smart effects are to be as popular as ever"[30]). After the advertisements for real estate, insurance, and auto shuttle service, readers found a synopsis of the current week's feature: *The Wife*. "Probably the greatest of all the Belasco-DeMille plays is *The Wife*," the column reads. "It is a story of contemporary Washington life, dealing largely in politics and using an innocent woman as a tool to further the ends of scheming politicians."[31]

The scheming wasn't just happening in visual fiction. The power play between Jacksonville and Los Angeles had reached a fever pitch. In 1914, the United States Film Corporation announced its plan to move to Jacksonville. Its statement read, "There is no tangible reason why Jacksonville should not reap the same benefits as Los Angeles. Very few realize the enormous investments made in Los Angeles or the wonderful returns that have accrued, as great as 3,000 percent."[32]

Two years later, Jacksonville officially put Los Angeles in its crosshairs.

In early 1916, there were an estimated 16,000 theaters nationwide, most of which were located in Florida and California. But that year, there were some rumblings in California that had nothing to do with the San Andreas Fault. Los Angeles—the city, the businesses, the people—had become a nuisance to local filmmakers. Shops had raised the prices of their goods and services. Clergymen had joined reformers in attacking the moral standing of show business. The Los Angeles City Council had even proposed an ordinance that would have separated the studios from the city's residential areas.

In *Movie-Made America*, Robert Sklar captures the attitudes toward the Los Angeles studios. "As far as the local residents were concerned, the motion picture people were in Los Angeles and Hollywood, but not of them. Migrants to Southern California came preponderantly from the South and Midwest, and brought with them strong strains of fundamentalist condemnation of popular amusements and the theater. They called the studios 'camps'; it was a good name in the sense that studio life was self-contained and isolated from the community, a bad one if they thought the motion-picture interlopers would pack up and go away."[33]

The studios did not stand by idly. "Hopes of Floridians that the state would continue to flourish were further spurred when more than 100 companies located in California threatened to move unless proposed censorship ordinances and 'petty restrictions' enacted by city and state officials there were rescinded."[34]

Jacksonville pounced on the wounded animal. On the morning of January 16, the *Florida Times-Union* printed the following headline: "Delegation May Be Sent To New York To Get California Motion Picture Industries." The lobbying group, which included city officials and members of the Chamber of Commerce and the Tourist and Convention Bureau, believed that attracting California's studios "will pour at least $30,000,000 annually into local coffers and increase the resident population by over 6,000 persons." The previous evening, the delegation and representatives from several local studios, including Thanhouser, Eagle, and Metro, had met at the Hotel Mason to discuss the matter. The *Florida Times-Union* reported that Metro's spokesperson, an unnamed director, "found Florida without handicaps existing in California and especially about Los Angeles, where he said foggy weather almost daily made picture making an impossibility for any continuous length of time." The director added that "he was most favorably impressed because of the short distance between Jacksonville and New York by boat or rail and the bright light effects continuing throughout the morning and into the afternoon."[35]

But Jacksonville had its own hindrances to work through. While there were many production companies in town, quite a few had taken residence in vacant buildings not built for filmmaking. The old warehouses, barns, yacht clubs, and so forth were not built with lighting, space, and accessibility in mind. Another issue was film processing—there was no dedicated facility to develop the huge amount of stock shot in Jacksonville. Companies had to shoot the film, package it, send it on a northbound train to New York, have it processed, and then have it shipped back to Florida for editing.

Then Richard Garrick showed up with his Big Idea. Garrick, former producer with the Gaumont Players, the French company that had worked from Dixieland Park for a spell, had recently established his own company, Garrick Studios Company. In July 1916, he announced plans to create a modern film campus. "Richard Garrick, the well-known motion picture producer and director . . . will commence erection of the second largest general studio in America. . . . It has resulted in commendatory expressions and much speculation as to the ultimate possibilities for the studio eclipsing even the famous Universal City, which from the beginning will be its only peer."[36]

The five-acre complex would accommodate twenty film companies with its 67,000 square feet of floor space and would feature a complete processing laboratory, 100 dressing rooms, carpentry shops, restaurant, and a garage filled with cars for use in the movies. The structure would be built atop the Union Terminal Building on Union Street. To underscore his seriousness, Garrick secured a 99-year lease on the building.[37]

According to the *Florida Times-Union*, "the capacity of the studio will be for twenty companies each averaging ten principals and about one hundred supers. With every available portion of rental space taken and the full number of companies operating, a minimum of between 2,200 and 2,500 persons would be here: and every one of them spending parts of their salaries in Jacksonville." Any parties nervous about cutting the umbilical cord to Manhattan kept the Garrick Studio Company's promotional slogan in mind: "Only 27 Hours from Broadway."[38]

And so it happened—a textbook second-act conflict. Two competing entities clashing for power, money, and billing. Any Hollywood star can tell you the importance of billing: where your name physically appears on the movie's promotional materials. Better to be above the title than below; better to be on the left than the right. Jacksonville and Hollywood were competing for star billing.

⊰ 6 ⊱

The Movie Mayor

As executive of Jacksonville, Fla., I extend
to the moving picture fraternity of this country
a cordial invitation to our city.

—J.E.T. Bowden

Finding information about J.E.T. Bowden is not easy. His legacy is like Hansel and Gretel's bread-crumb trail—you trace it crumb by crumb. His name most often appears as a bookmark for the Jacksonville mayors he preceded or succeeded. Look for him and you'll find John Martin, who after serving Jacksonville's municipality went on to be the twenty-fourth governor of Florida. You'll also find John T. Alsop, the mayor whose name is still recognized thanks to the Alsop Memorial Bridge that spans the St. Johns and connects downtown to Springfield. Bowden doesn't quite get the same treatment. But if you're looking for Queen of Sheba, the only Ethiopian restaurant in town, you'll find it on Bowden Road.

Bowden is also a difficult name to put a face to. Few photographs are available of him. In the Florida Photographic Collection of the State Archives of Florida, home to some 850,000 images, there is only one image of Bowden, an illustration of a young man with a bristly moustache and cresting wave of brown curls. The most commonly found image is a black-and-white portrait from his later years. In the undated photo, Bowden is soft and ashen. With his white coif and brittle frame, polar irises and pale skin, he brings to mind a snowman after a two-day warm front.

You search for Bowden because he is one of the most important figures in Jacksonville history. He was a hugely successful businessman, for a time one of the largest real estate proprietors in the city. He was mayor, among many other roles, during the Great Fire of 1901. And most relevant to this story, he was the city's biggest film booster, a fiery politician who used his power to help the industry gain its foothold during the 1910s. From scraps to ephemera to old photos of old photos, this is the trail to J.E.T. Bowden, the movie mayor.

༘ ༚

James Edmund Thomas Bowden was born on September 14, 1857. As was the case for many in those days, war framed many aspects of his life. His hometown was Spartanburg, South Carolina, a city named for the American Revolutionary forces known as the "Spartan Rifles" who helped defeat the British at the Battle of Cowpens in 1781. His father, John Ramsey Bowden, served in the Confederate army as a physician.

Following the Union's victory, John took his family south to Gainesville in 1867. He decided to start a business, entering the mercantile and cotton trades. But the soldier's entrepreneurial skills proved inept, and a year later the business failed and the family was left destitute. On June 20, 1869, the Bowdens cut east across the scrub, eventually settling in Jacksonville.[1]

Young James participated in Duval County's educational system, attending Duval High School. But he was also drawn—by interest or duty, one is not sure—to the work force. At age 10 he was selling newspapers. A job with a printing house followed, where he spent his afternoons and evenings with the rumbling presses. When he was 13, Bowden was hired as a cash boy (think bipedal cash register) for the popular department store Furchgott-Benedict & Company. Turns as salesman and head clerk followed shortly thereafter.[2]

In 1881, at the ripe age of 24, Bowden opened a general store with his savings of $2,000. The store was located at 11 West Bay Street, a stretch known mostly for its tourist-magnet novelty shops. By 1887, the business was worth $50,000.[3] He parlayed that capital into real estate, becoming an owner, renter, and landlord of more than 200 properties.[4]

It was no secret to the LaVilla locals that Bowden was one of the area's largest landowners. He was known as something of a character, a lethal combination of pinstriped spitfire and dulcet orator. He was not afraid to mix it up and dish it out. "Bowden smoked cigars and drank a lot of coffee. He had a temper and could cuss like a sailor."[5] It was these qualities that led him to be elected mayor of LaVilla in 1886. His first order of business was chasing out the police and aldermen from their murky bog of local corruption. "He denounced the aldermen as 'drunkards and barroom pimps . . . who have not the least regard for their oaths of office,'" and said that "'for a drink of whiskey . . . they would sell their votes for any purpose.'"[6] A year later, the municipality of LaVilla was placed under the jurisdiction of the city of Jacksonville, and Bowden was out of a job.

He was anything but quiet during his years in the private sector. In fact, he was a press-magnet chatterbox for Jacksonville's biggest sports controversy of all time: "Gentleman" Jim Corbett, boxing champion of America, verses Charles Mitchell, boxing champion of England.

Getting clocked in the face for money was a crime. Like a human cockfight, the boxing matches of the early twentieth century involved throwing two bare-knucklers on a floating San Francisco dock or into a backwoods Boston barn and letting the fists fly and the gambling pot swell until the police showed up with the paddy wagon. The fighters were mostly Irish or Polish thicknecks with names like Sullivan, Choynski, O'Donnell, and McDonald, men who made their reputation as lumberjacks, loggers, or sideshow strongmen. Much of that changed with the arrival of James J. Corbett. A former bank clerk known for his sharp dress and impeccable pompadour, Corbett gave prizefighting a glint of sophistication—just a glint, mind you. Don't let the nickname *Gentleman* fool you; this was a hard-boiled fighter stocked with blood and guts. On May 21, 1891, Corbett fought Peter "Black Prince" Jackson. The contest ended in a draw after sixty-one rounds.

And so in 1893, the world's two greatest fighters were looking for a venue to settle an international score: Old Glory in the blue-and-red trunks, Union Jack in the blue-and-white trunks. The *Evening Telegraph*, a British newspaper, made the announcement official with a wire it received from the Duval Athletic Club in Jacksonville: "Final arrangements have been completed for a glove contest between Corbett and Mitchell. . . . The purse is $20,000 and there are side bets of $10,000 each. . . . All hands have signed the papers and the thing is settled."[7]

The event became Jacksonville's first sports extravaganza. Historian John Cowart writes, "In the following weeks, over 300 newspapers converged on Jacksonville to cover the fight. . . . Most newspapers used line drawings to illustrate their coverage. . . . Through Western Union, the sports reporters wired an estimated three million words to their respective papers. Most were fighting words."[8]

These weren't just fighting words for the sake of pugilism. A new battle was under way, one that traded gloves and grease for legalese and scripture. There were two sides to this fight. Churches, government officials, and civic groups were set on preventing this immoral contest from taking place on local soil. And the self-named "Sports," a glorified gang of fight supporters, proclaimed that the heavyweight championship of the world—the *world*—would be named in their town.

The Sports were a dandy of a group, an assemblage of entrepreneurs with money to burn, notorious athletes, inventors, gamblers, and bootleggers. Cowart rattles off the Sports' roster, which reads like a VIP list to purgatory:

> Bat Masterson, gunslinger; Henry Stedker, New York bookmaker; . . . Kit Muller, an all around good fellow and one of the most popular traveling men who do Florida in the interests of houses that sell the nectar of white corn; . . . Snapper Garrison, noted jockey; . . . H. B. Perkins, popular mixologist of the St. James Hotel; 100 members of the East End Club of London; Inspector McLaughlin of the New York Police Force; H. B. Miner, well known theatrical man; Johnny Ward, the great baseball manager; . . . George Smith, better known as "Pittsburgh Phil," the famous plunger who has won thousands of dollars on the race track; and Professor C. R. Ramsey, inventor and patentee of Ramsey's new and improved punching bag.[9]

Nominated to speak for the Sports was none other than J.E.T. Bowden.

The Sports' opposition, by contrast, was a white-collar who's who. At the top was Henry Laurens Mitchell, the former Florida Supreme Court justice and current governor of Florida. From there it trickled down to the Honorable Henry I. Mitchell, the sheriff of Duval County; troops in the Second

Battalion of Ocala Rifles and Florida State Militia; and members of the local humane society. Their moral ground was that they were speaking for the "moral element in this country."[10] Their legal ground was that dueling was illegal in the state of Florida.

Bowden's position surrounded the facts without really touching the issue. "We do not propose to have a prize fight, or anything like a fight, and my efforts in drawing up contracts, etc., have been with that one object to eliminate everything pertaining to a fight and to only have a scientific glove contest, pure and simple." Through a statement from the city attorney, Jacksonville mayor Duncan U. Fletcher counter-punched. "Members of the city government say that they are law-abiding and God-fearing and that a prize fight, although cloaked as a 'scientific glove contest' will not be tolerated within the confines of their official jurisdiction if there be any legal method of preventing it."[11]

Others began piling on. The East Coast Conference of Congregational Churches used the words *disgraceful* and *demoralizing*. The Humane Society of St. Augustine used high-falutin' rhetoric: "We hereby express our abhorrence of and opposition to all pugilistic encounters!"

When a location for the fight was being discussed and places outside city limits became an option, a disgruntled elder statesman made a statement. Henry Flagler, the man who had made Jacksonville accessible, was now intent on making it inaccessible. The January 17 edition of the *Florida Times-Union* reported that "Mr. Flagler will use all his influence to checkmate any movement that the club may make to have fighters adjourn to the country in which his hotels are located. . . . He does not want it held in Florida. . . . He thinks the bad name it will give the state will injure the whole of it."[12] When word floated north that the fight might migrate to Georgia, governor W. J. Northern shipped crates of 300 extra rifles to the Fifth Georgia Cavalry in Waycross, a small town sixty-six miles northwest of Fernandina Beach.[13]

More characters began showing up at the gates of goodness and decency, one of the most bombastic being Napoleon Bonaparte Broward, the Jacksonville sheriff ordered by the governor to stop the fight. Interestingly, Broward would anger Governor Mitchell later that year by placing deputies at the voting precincts to prevent the time-honored tradition of vote-buying. Governor Mitchell removed him from office, citing him for "unlawfully interfering with state elections." In 1904, Broward was elected governor by 600 votes.

The law was now fully involved in this donnybrook—Governor Mitchell had mobilized the Duval County sheriffs and local militiamen. But the Sports would not stand down. Bowden swore to the people of Jacksonville that the fight would go on and the military would not interfere. Bowden even got support from his former employer, L. Furchgott, owner of Furchgott-Benedict & Company, who protested the acts of the governor and called the presence of armed enforcers unwarranted.

It all came down to a showdown of another sort at the state capital. Following the meeting, each released their own statement to the press and both used the same wording: the situation is unchanged.

The tiebreaker came down to Circuit Court judge H. M. Call. He issued an injunction against Sheriff Broward, dictating that no soldier would trespass on club property and that no interference with the prizefight would take place.

On January 25, 1894, at 2:30 p.m., a bell rang ringside at the makeshift arena in Moncrief Park, now a low-income area west of I-95. Approximately 1,800 people were on hand for the fight. By-the-round updates were sent worldwide via wire; some out-of-town venues had acrobats and gymnasts reenact the flight blow by blow. In just three rounds, the fight was over. This was the official play-by-play of that final round:

ROUND THREE: Mitchell groggy. Corbett rushed at him swinging right and left to the neck. Mitchell went down. Mitchell took full time to rise. Corbett rushed at him like a tiger. Mitchell clinched. Corbett threw him off and floored him with a stiff facer. Again Mitchell took the full time to rise and when he advanced to Corbett, the latter swung his right with deadly effect to Mitchell's nose. Mitchell reeled and fell on his face, helpless—knocked out.[14]

According to Davis, "No attempt was made to stop the fight during its progress, but both Corbett and Mitchell were arrested immediately afterward. Each was released on $5,000 bond."[15]

In 1899, Bowden decided to take the city into the twentieth century by joining the mayoral race. He faced incumbent William D. Knight in the primary. The campaign's key issue was prohibition: Knight was taking the

Methodist high road, Bowden the realist's center. "As long as man is endowed with the nature that he possesses[,] these evils cannot be wholly eradicated," Bowden said during one campaign speech.[16]

Bowden, whose speaking skills were a mix of conviction and jabberwocky, was the first to admit enjoying such vices, even taking a populist's stand on its enjoyment. "I belong to a club where at the tap of a bell at any hour of the day or any minute in the hour, on Sunday or any other day, I can order any kind of liquor I desire," Bowden announced from the podium of the Park Opera House. "The poor man cannot have this privilege, but I do not think it is right that I, or any man, because he is rich, should have privileges that he would deny to the poor man."[17]

Unfortunately for Knight, he was the biggest detriment to his own campaign. In a refreshing bit of self-flagellating honesty, Knight told a group of black voters, "I did not come here to make a speech, as I am dodging the issues that some are trying to bring up."[18]

In the June 8 primary, Bowden won in a landslide over Knight, although in this small town, the landslide was more of an eroding molehill: Bowden got 907 votes and Knight got 687. After the polls closed, Bowden was met by his constituency in the streets and was carried triumphantly down Bay Street, where his ascent to city dignitary began.[19] Two weeks later he won the general election by a margin of 3 to 1.

Little did Mayor J.E.T. Bowden know that in less than two years, he would face a challenger far tougher than Governor Mitchell or Sheriff Broward. He would be chasing a dragon from his city.

⧜

On May 3, 1901, Mayor Bowden was in his home, a stucco wedding cake in posh Riverside, with twenty of the Great Fire's 10,000 refugees. It looked like nighttime—the smoke had been choking out the sunlight for hours. Bowden had spent his day crisscrossing the city through the ashy smog, checking on friends, family, and citizens and following the blaze like a storm chaser. He was "wearied in body but with his indomitable spirit in full working order."[20] From his house that night, Bowden scheduled a 10:30 a.m. meeting with all the heads of the city's municipal government bodies at the offices of the *Florida Times-Union*.

The next day, the *Florida Metropolis* reported, "Mayor Bowden Alive!"

"The mayor was one of the busiest men in the city yesterday, and at one time it was reported that a building had fallen on him. He turned up, however, this morning without a scratch, and is working with a vim to rebuild the city."[21]

In his morning meeting, Bowden delegated responsibilities: receiving and distributing food and clothing to the needy by the Commissary Department, handling donations and approving expenditures by the Finance Committee, and identifying lost homes and property for the Bureau of Information. Bowden himself headed up the Bureau of Transportation, securing transport for those anxious to leave town. At the same time, he was adamant about establishing a sense of normalcy amid the chaos. Mail must be delivered, electricity restored, water and sewer services repaired.

With information disseminating at the speed of Western Union, Bowden made it a priority to redirect the flow of tourists away from the city. Railway cars filled with blissfully ignorant vacationers were turned away. "Beg the people to stay away," Bowden pled to the *Jacksonville Journal*. "We have no room for our own—everything is gone." Bowden's pathos also surfaced in his plea for help. "The United States is too big a country and her people too good to permit us to starve to death."[22]

This doesn't mean the mayor had lost his fiery scruples. In H. L. Mencken's recollection of the Great Fire, he mentions a few choice encounters with Hizzoner, one referring to the City of Baltimore's inexplicable donations of 100 second-hand horse blankets and 100 cases of rye.

"When I took these dispatches to the Mayor of Jacksonville I expected (at least officially) that he would burst into tears and bid me thank the good people of Baltimore for their generosity, but what he actually did was laugh," writes Mencken. "I must confess that, at the thought of the horse-blankets, I had to smile myself, for the temperature in Jacksonville was rising 80 degrees." He later adds that it was the Maryland rye that "really flabbergasted the Mayor. He was far from a Prohibitionist, but the fire had given him plenty of worries, and he did not welcome the new one provided by those 100 cases of rye."[23]

For the weeks and months that followed the fire, Bowden was everywhere and anywhere, working so hard that he fell ill several times. In one case a local doctor diagnosed him as "delirious." When his two-year term ended in June of that same year, Bowden bowed out, citing exhaustion. This was an unfortunate turn of events because, as Foley and Wood put it, "he was at the zenith of his popularity, having led Jacksonville through its worst disaster."[24] His successor was Duncan U. Fletcher, the mayor of Jacksonville during the Corbett-Mitchell debacle.

⊰ ⊱

For the first time in a long time he had free time, and free time didn't work so well for Bowden. He still had his projects—real estate and such—but he stumbled through a series of new business ventures. He started the first taxi company in Florida. When the business failed, he had the chauffeurs drive the cabs into the St. Johns. He also opened a spa. It opened one night and burned down the next.

In 1915, the prodigal candidate returned to open arms. He again ran for mayor and in the primary met incumbent Van Swearingen, a Democrat with a lust for public decency. He was known for ordering policemen to clear the streets of prostitutes and condemning the giant nude paintings that were de rigueur at most of the town's saloons and taverns. Bowden beat Van Swearingen in the primary, taking 58 percent of the vote, and then soundly defeated Socialist candidate I. C. Baldwin in the general election. Bowden's campaign was powered by the slogan "Just Easy Times, Boys," a gutsy motto for a city—and country—battling recession.

Bowden was elected into the thick of the film industry's growth. In this industry, where studios paid millions for labor, talent, and production and the audiences paid millions for laughs, scares, and surprises, Bowden saw a boost for the local economy and used his political clout to support it by any means possible. He asked residents to submit recommendations for shooting locations. He also wasn't afraid to walk a red carpet. The Gaumont film *The Idol of the Stage*, directed by Richard Garrick, used more than 1,000 locals as extras. At the premiere of the film held at the Prince Theater, Bowden met with the cast and crew and introduced them from the stage. However, Bowden didn't go as far as some local officials: William Meyers, mayor of South Jacksonville, was employed as an extra in several Gaumont pictures.

Bowden's power move in luring studios from the West Coast came on January 12, 1916, when the *Florida Times-Union* announced that local civic and commercial leaders "are preparing to withdraw over one hundred producing companies from Los Angeles, because of unsuitable conditions which are said to have arisen there." The story's subtitle: "The Initial Gun Is Fired."[25]

At six o'clock that evening, Bowden presided over a meeting in the lobby of the Hotel Mason that included local leaders, businessmen, industry boosters, and representatives from local production companies (among them Kalem, Eagle, Metro, and Equitable). On the evening's agenda: making Jacksonville attractive to film companies and, as a result, making Los Angeles unattractive. H. H. Richardson, head of the Tourism and Convention Bureau, noted that Jacksonville "is exactly 2,149 miles nearer New York, from where all the releases are made and where is located the main offices and factories of the producers, than Los Angeles."[26]

Richardson sent a telegram to Mack Sennett, head of the successful Keystone Film Company, best known for their "Keystone Kops" shorts. Richardson's telegram had the hook of a sales pitch and the drama of a great DeMille picture. "In looking for a new location you are urged to carefully investigate and consider Jacksonville, the hospitable Southern city, the metropolis of Florida, a state whose history is filled with the romance of the past and citizenship will give you a typical Southern and sunny welcome." One wonders if the telegram had clearly targeted the right person or if the name *Mack Sennett* was blindly written over an address. "The Initial Gun Is Fired In The Dark" may have been a more suitable subtitle. Evidence to that point appears in the telegram's salutation: "Please pass on to interested parties."[27]

Bowden one-upped Harrison's close-eyes-and-shoot approach. He sent a telegram to the Photo Players' Screen Club of Los Angeles, the acting and directing guild for the entire city. It reads as follows:

> As executive of Jacksonville, Fla., I extend to the moving picture fraternity of this country a cordial invitation to our city. I pledge you every consideration that is possible. You will find atmospheric conditions suitable for work necessary to carry on moving picture business. Many companies located here now. Am told by those connected with them static conditions are superior to any other portion of the country. Our magnificent streams, tropical foliage, in fact, every condition necessary except mountain scenery obtained here. Earnestly request investigation.[28]

A year later, in 1917, it was time for Mayor Bowden to again run for office, and he had the whole of the film industry supporting him. A campaign party hosted by composer George M. Cohan, whose life was dramatized in the 1942 James Cagney vehicle *Yankee Doodle Dandy*, was held for Bowden at the Burbridge Hotel. Babe Hardy threw his own election soiree for Bowden at the Mason Hotel, just down the block from the Duval Theatre. But all the ticker tape and confetti couldn't mask what was happening. Bowden, the industry, the lot of them, were losing their grip. The future was an old single-reel film with botched sprocket holes—unsettled, washed out, quaking violently across the illuminated filament.

❈ 7 ❈

The Boom Goes Boom

A great city tumbling to the tune of a cranking camera . . .
—*Florida Times-Union*, January 4, 1916

Even the firemen were cast in action films by Kalem and Lubin, particularly the members of the Number Six Hose Company. There they were, all forklift jawlines and curly moustaches, being called "to hitch up and head out at a dead run as if they were on the way to a general alarm. The firehorses would breathe down the exhaust of a tonneau car speeding ahead of them with a camera mounted on the rear."[1]

Others benefited too. Hotels like the Burbridge were regularly booked with stars and film crews. For furniture stores like Furchgott's on Adams Street, renting became big business as the studios constantly rotated its furnishings: an armoire and bed for the love scene at night; a wicker dining set for the ladies' tea the next morning. A new railway station was under way that would make it possible for even more undeveloped film stock, costumes, and equipment to shuttle between Jacksonville and Manhattan.

Jacksonville was getting quite a reputation. It had been dubbed "The World's Winter Film Capital"; others knew it as "The Motion Picture Producing Mecca of the Atlantic Coast." In September 1916, the *Florida Metrop-*

olis announced that the Union Street Railway Terminal, set to be upstaged by the new Parthenon on Riverside Avenue, was being converted into "the largest studio in the world, and second only to Universal in California in size."[2] (The studio was never built.)

Energized by the producers' blustery gospel, the newspaper columnist became both Jacksonville's biggest fan and the finger in Los Angeles' ribcage. The *Florida Metropolis* published this in the spring of 1916:

> The time has arrived where no State or city which has the natural advantages can afford to ignore the fostering of business with motion pictures companies. The moving picture industry today is the third biggest in the whole United States, being exceeded in importance as regards to money and income by only the steel and oil industries. . . . It is likely to be one of the biggest factors in the future prosperity of Florida, a factor which gives us an endless amount of free advertising, which is worth millions of dollars to the State.[3]

Just as Jacksonville was beginning to find success as a filmmaking town, the city was beset by problems. If you rewind and freeze frame in Chapter 5, you can glimpse the descent's genesis. Look for the Belgian-made Fabrique Nationale M 1910 semi-automatic pistol exploding smoothly in Sarajevo.

The Archduke Franz Ferdinand, heir to the Austro-Hungarian throne, arrived in Bosnia with trepidation. His empire had been viewed as Machiavellian, and many in Serbia had become dissidents under its thumb. The archduke and his pregnant wife Sophia Chotek made the trip nonetheless. The plan was pleasant enough. Ferdinand and his wife would take part in a hand-waving motorcade through Sarajevo. The two would ride in the archduke's mint-condition Graf und Stift, the first Austrian-made motorcar. The motorcade's route placed the Sarajevo faithful on one side and the scenic River Miljacka on the other.

Ferdinand avoided disaster on the way to his tour speech—a stick of dynamite was tossed at the car but missed—but he couldn't escape fate on his way out. While the car was being driven away, a bullet pierced the metal above the right rear wheel and hit Sophie in the stomach. The bullet that followed caught Ferdinand in the neck. The motorcade sped off, the two left sitting upright, dying in their seats.

This is the famous tragedy that instigated World War I. The trickle became a ripple that became a roar, a tsunami breaking slowly across the world. It finally hit Jacksonville in 1917 when the United States officially entered World War I. For the locals in Jacksonville, the reality hit home "when the port commissioners placed the German steamship Freda Leonardt under surveillance for an alleged statement by her crew that in the event of war they would blow up the municipal electric plant here."[4]

For filmmakers, war had important ramifications. With the U.S. entry into World War I, railroads were redirected to handle war supplies, leaving the film studios to find alternate means of transport. Local export businesses watched their goods rot on the docks, as trade to Europe had essentially ceased. The loss of personnel to the war was also a problem. In the late 1970s, the *Jacksonville Journal* acquired the handwritten notes of Glen Lambert, a Richmond-born writer-director who spent much of his career in Jacksonville. Lambert wrote that World War I "killed Jacksonville's film industry." He added, "The picture business was shot. Many of the actors and technicians joined the armed forces, while others went to Hollywood where the industry was booming."[5]

Some industries profited from the war, most notably shipbuilding. Frederick Davis, historian of Jacksonville, wrote that "the Government's pre-war survey of the possibility of ship-building in the Jacksonville vicinity resulted favorably and within a few weeks after war was declared several firms had received ship-building orders." Between July 1918 and July 1919, fifteen ships were constructed in Jacksonville, their total weight 62,000 tons. Soon the St. Johns ports were filled with 3,500- and 6,000-ton steamers with names like *Apalachee, Fort Lauderdale, Fort Pierce, Wekika,* and *Pinellas.* The labor needs of the shipbuilding industry siphoned people from the film industry's fringe workforce, those hangers-on looking to make scratch as extras, techs, stuntmen, and gophers. Davis added that "as soon as the shipyards were opened, labor flocked to them, attracted by the relatively enormous wages offered almost any and everybody."[6]

Inside the ports and shipyards, workers were making money hand over fist. Their fleeting wealth translated into a lot of disposable income, which they spent lavishly. This spending raised the city's cost of living; rents increased, as did the cost of fuel and electricity. The cost of clothing and furniture also increased. In 1918, "men's clothing was 199 percent and women's apparel averaged 226 percent above the 1914 prices. . . . According to the Government's report, Jacksonville rose to the rank of fifth in the list of American cities with respect to the high cost of living at the time."[7]

The film industry accused some of the suppliers of price-gouging. Frederick Davis reported, "Mass-meetings were held to devise means for combating it and general boycotts were suggested. The charge against merchants of profiteering was often heard, but in most cases the charge was unjust, for their troubles were as great as others."[8]

But the rising cost of living was only one aspect of economic change during the war. The city, and nation, was also battling a business depression and low wages. In 1917 the U.S. Food Administration started a "food pledge campaign," in which families signed pledge cards promising to conserve food by using substitutes, particularly sugar and flour, "in order that the 'boys' in uniform might not be denied these." The days were marked like holidays in purgatory. There were "wheatless" days where no flour was sold. "Meatless" days followed suit. "Lightless" days, where the city shut down sections of its grid to conserve fuel, came sporadically, announced with the innocuous calm of church bells.[9]

The film industry was part of the problem. Its wages were fairly low. Extras were paid next to nothing just for the chance to be in the movies. In New York, pay for extras ran between $8 and $10 a day. In Jacksonville, it was less than half that, roughly $3 to $5 for a day's work.[10]

Jacksonville's film boom, its Gold Rush of rushes, so to speak, attracted a new element. Like the northern carpetbaggers that came South during Reconstruction, Jacksonville's film industry had its share of charlatan capitalists from the North looking to get a piece of the lights, camera, action. For every decent and respectable film company that came to Jacksonville, there were two dozen fly-by-night filmmakers known as "piker promoters." They would rush into town, wander along Main Street, and offer investment opportunities to passers-by, promising riches from their soon-to-be-shot blockbuster. The practice became so rampant that in April 1916 representatives from the city's established studios issued a public warning about these "stock jobbers."[11]

But who was going to save the city's "approved" filmmakers from themselves? Their practices became increasingly crass and roughshod, turning the townscape into one large set where the suspension of disbelief extended into the realms of law and good taste. For the 1916 film *The Dead Alive*, written and directed by Henry Vernot and produced by Gaumont, an automobile race was staged through Main Street, ending with the car plunging off a ferry dock into the St. Johns. It was the last shot of the movie, in case anyone in the cast didn't recover.[12]

That's just only one of many examples. As in every other southern town, Sunday in Jacksonville was for church and prayer—saloons and movie theaters weren't open on the Sabbath. That didn't stop the rogue filmmakers from staging bank robberies while the streets were empty. This drew the ire of Jacksonville's huge population of churchgoers.

Sometimes locals were cast in films without their consent. Fire alarms were pulled when filmmakers needed to shoot fire engines. One moviemaker advertised a parachute jump from the Graham Building, the fifteen-story tower on West Forsyth Street that was once the tallest building in the city, in order to draw a crowd.[13]

But the biggest debacle, the one that derailed support for the film industry, the one that became the we-told-you-so platform for politicians and reformers, took place on a chilly January morning shortly after New Year's Day, 1916. The film was an adaptation of a recent novel about an anti-establishment newspaper. On the day's shooting schedule: a mob scene.

In his 1914 novel *The Clarion*, Samuel Hopkins Adams chose to focus on his own trade—the newspaper business—and depict the fate of independent-minded publications that fight against imposed consensus. The title refers to the fictional *Worthington Daily Clarion*, the controversial publication at the center of the novel. At the end of the book, protagonist Harrington "Hal" Surtaine, editor of the paper, holes up in his headquarters to ward off the attack of an angry mob. The book's charged plotline and dramatic conclusion caught the attention of the Equitable Film Company, and they adapted it into a six-reel drama.

The Clarion's mob scene was scheduled to shoot in the first days of January 1916. The scene called for a large crowd, and for several days Equitable manager Clifford Robertson "put advertisements in the *Florida Times-Union* calling for men and boys as well as a specified number of women, whom he wanted to form a mob." The would-be extras came in droves, as they always did in Jacksonville. "So great was the number answering the call that it was necessary to open a temporary office in the [Hotel] Mason arcade." In the script, the extras were referred to as "general medley of humanity."[15]

Robertson had secured a place willing to host the riot scene, a two-story brick saloon on Davis Street that would double for the *Worthington Daily Clarion's* headquarters. Perhaps star-struck by the movie magic or lured by the chance for free advertising, the saloon's owner made the strangest agreement: he gave the extras "the privilege of smashing every window in his place as well as the stock of liquor on display in the front end." The mob extras were told the hour when they should report "for their destructive work."[16]

When the clapboard sounded, the cameras—some set up as far as several hundred feet away—began to roll, thousands of feet of unexposed stock at the ready. Director James Durkin gave the signal and the mob rushed down the street "hurling bricks, sticks and every missile they could find." Once it reached the saloon, the mob became, well, a mob. They rushed into the bar and while destroying the place, imbibed from the bottles of wine and whiskey left out as props. "In some instances, it is said, they were so eager to get at the choice fluids within that they snapped off the necks and flung away the glass encased corks (actually) without ado."[17]

Forty policemen were on hand but not on duty. Like the Number Six Hose Company before them, they were here to be immortalized in celluloid. Instead of regulating the reality, they joined the fiction. "The forty members . . . were supposed . . . to rush madly about wielding clubs with alacrity in an effort to quell the disturbance. The clubs were rubber, however, and the bluecoats got five bucks each for not hurting anybody." At this point, the film already had an audience—a crowd of rubberneckers had gathered on the street. Unlike those that would see *The Clarion* in theaters later that year, this audience watched the unfolding scene in color. As the real/fake mob was beaten by the real/fake police with real/fake batons, "maybe the accumulating crowd of spectators along the sidewalk and at street crossings thought the mob was an awful hard-headed one. But, shucks, who cares? It was only the movies."[18]

On January 4, 1916, the *Florida Times-Union* ran the headline: "Mob Destroys Brick Building on Davis Street and then Wrecks a Saloon." The structure was toppled, the windows were shattered, and the saloon "was deprived of . . . a good quantity of choice liquors." The Equitable Film Company paid the $2,000 bill.[19]

But the sensational event—liquor, anger, anarchy, annihilation, civil servants who surrendered their sworn duty to the barrel of a Bell & Howell hand-crank camera—portended an inevitable fate. Everyone could see it coming. Even the newspaper columnists, once loyal disciples, changed their tune. "Although Jacksonville, for the past several months, has been gradually becoming the motion picture manufacturing center of the Atlantic seaboard, she has never before been the place for such scenes of violence committed in the name of silent drama," read a *Florida Times-Union* article. It went on to say that if the first-person accounts of *The Clarion* debacle were accurate, it "would have resulted in the depiction of a great city tumbling to the tune of a cranking camera silently turned by a practical operator."[20]

One year later, a mayoral election ended the honeymoon once and for all.

≈§≈

Jacksonville's biggest film booster was preparing for the biggest race of his career. The man who had seen the city through the Great Fire, been to election parties hosted by Oliver Hardy, and invited citizens to submit prospective filmmaking locations ran for mayor for the third time in 1917. His party opponent was Democrat John Wellborn Martin. Martin's political pedigree was of a different make than Bowden's. While Bowden was the garrulous craggy pontificator, Martin was a polished round-faced aristocrat with America in his blood. His ancestors included John Martin, who had come to Virginia with Captain John Smith in 1607, and Abram Martin, who had served under General George Washington in the French and Indian War.[21]

Martin was only 33 when he threw his hat in the ring, but he came out of his corner like a bull. He called Bowden out for his lax treatment of the corrupt film industry. He chastised him for taking campaign funds raised by the city's top movie producers and allowing these entities to have a say in the city's politics. Bowden took his rebuttal to the pages of the *Florida Times-Union* in a paid political advertisement titled "To the People of Jacksonville":

> I did interest, among other industries, a rich, thrifty, cultured and delightful community of incoming producers of moving picture film companies and players . . . . I feel a just satisfaction in this, and a recent

suggestion from the stump that our new citizenship of the film world might take an undue interest in city politics appears to me rather ungracious and uncalled for. . . . Can we afford to ignore and disparage a cash payroll of from $40,000 to $50,000 a week from the film industry in order to exclude some mighty good new citizenship from our midst?[22]

But Martin didn't relent. In the last week of the campaign, he went to the streets with his offensive. On February 4th, the *Florida Times-Union* reported that "[Martin] drove from place to place and spoke to the voters at several different corners during the evening, despite the cold weather."[23] Martin must have been encouraged by a paid editorial that ran in the paper that day. The Woman's Club of Jacksonville was announcing plans to create its own purified motion picture circuit. The article stated that the Woman's Club was "endeavoring to establish a number of motion picture circuits throughout the state for special children's pictures in the effort to secure positively accredited pictures for children's matinees, and we are writing to ask your cooperation and assistance in doing this."[24]

Martin's political advertisements in the local newspapers announced his qualifications: "He Has Used Only Clean and Upright Campaign Methods," "He Has Nothing to Sell to the City" and "He Is a Candidate of No Clique or Faction—But of All Classes." It was a veiled critique of Bowden, a man who had something to sell to the city through his insurance business and rental properties and was the candidate of the film clique and its supporting faction. Martin also accused Bowden of being a supporter of the Negro.

Bowden found himself on the defensive constantly and spent most of his time deflecting accusations, not making them. The barrage of jabs forced Bowden to once again retaliate in the papers, which he did in an absurdly lengthy article (more than 2,000 words) that responded to each of Martin's claims. He addressed the questions about his insurance business ("the books are open to any reputable committee that cares to examine them") and his relationship with the black community ("Mr. Martin has on many occasions attacked me as a negro lover, inciting the unthinking minds against me: insinuating that I had addressed the negroes of this city on familiar terms, and that I was making them my social equal. . . . These assertions are . . . LIES CUT FROM WHOLE CLOTH"). He went on to target Martin's mudslinging (he has "been vilifying me at every opportunity") and unsavory campaign tactics ("I have never known of a candidate being successful who tried to force himself into office over the corpse of his opponent").[25]

On February 7th, behind the Farm and Poultry section, the *Florida Times-Union* announced the results of the election. The headline read "John W. Martin Swept the City in the Contest for Mayor; Led J.E.T. Bowden by 834 Votes." Martin carried nine of the city's eleven wards. After the election, Martin said, "To my opponent I wish to express the pleasure I have felt in this association with him; and the hope that my friends will do all in their power to assist him to make the remainder of his term an unqualified success."[26]

Martin's anti-film administration was en route to power, and the reverberations were felt almost instantly in the film industry. Less than two weeks after the election, Richard Garrick announced he was leaving the city and closing his studios, which included abandoning his proposed studio project on Union Street. With the business depression still being felt, and the city's banks denying loans to filmmakers, more followed suit. Kalem left in March. Eagle foreclosed on its production space in Arlington. Firms like Selig, Edison, and Metro threw their weight behind operations up north and on the West Coast. Slowly but steadily everyone left town. For the first time in years, the perpetually booked Dixieland Studios had a "Space for Rent" sign.

One last black cloud arrived in 1918 with the flu epidemic. Jacksonville was used to periodic outbreaks of diseases. In 1883 there had been a smallpox outbreak. According to Frederick Davis, "About the middle of March, a negro sailor from New Orleans came ashore and stopped at a tenement house at Cedar and Forsyth Streets. He was sick at the time with smallpox, but before a diagnosis was made several colored people visited the place and contracted the disease. It spread and became a serious epidemic." Over the course of three months, 180 cases were treated, and one in three died. The yellow fever epidemic arrived five years later.[27]

The states had been passing influenza back and forth for the previous several years. There were reports that Florida, the tourist mecca that welcomed inbound germs by the trainload, might quarantine itself to stop an epidemic. Some didn't recommend such dramatic action. In 1916, state health officer Joseph Y. Porter said that Florida was practically immune from influenza. "The balmy air, the germ destroying sunshine and the tendency to not only live outdoors, but to sleep in well ventilated rooms or sleeping porches, restores vigor to the run down constitution and enabled the human system to ward off disease," said Dr. Porter, "One need not have influenza unless one wants to."[28]

In September 1918, a number of flu cases broke out among prisoners at a local work farm. "The disease gained momentum all over the city, so that by October 1st it was reported to the City Commission as being epidemic in Jacksonville." Volunteer nurses were called in. Newspapers ran inserts about influenza and its symptoms. A ban was placed on indoor public gatherings; the motion picture houses closed at the request of the superintendent of public instruction.[29]

By the end of October, the disease had infected some 30,000 Jacksonvillians, nearly the entire population. There were 464 reported deaths from influenza or its complication of pneumonia. It trailed off in 1919, but not before adding another 621 victims and 64 deaths.[30] The film industry suffered as well. During the epidemic, there was almost no audience for its films, and many of the city's movie theaters simply went out of business.

⁓§⁓

Like any good thriller, horror, or mystery, someone or something has to jump out during the third act for one last surprise. Henry Klutho was cast in that role. The architect who built metropolitan Jacksonville embarked on multiple last-ditch efforts to save the film industry.

In 1917, just as the movie mayor was packing up his office, the industry got a sliver of good news from an unlikely source. Klutho had decided to invest his own money in the construction of a state-of-the-art studio. How symbolic that the man who joined the city as it stood in ashes in 1902 would join the film industry as it faced a similar demise.

Klutho hoped his studio would do for the industry what the St. James Building had done for the city years earlier. "He has convinced himself that it will become necessary for Jacksonville to offer [the industry] greater facilities and advantages than are now possible," the *Florida Metropolis* reported. "With this in mind, he is seriously contemplating the erection of what will be one of the most modern studio buildings in the world."[31]

Henry J. Klutho, Jacksonville's most celebrated architect and fledgling film producer. *Florida Photographic Collection, Tallahassee, Florida*

Less than a week after the *Metropolis* report, construction began on Klutho Studios. Located on a huge parcel on the corner of Ninth and Main Streets, the complex's schematics called for two 50-by-80-foot outdoor studios covered with retractable sheets of muslin. (Waterproof canvases were also to be installed.) There were indoor studios, prop rooms, dressing rooms, offices, workshops, and projection rooms. The estimated cost was between $10,000 and $12,000.[32]

Pictures from the studio's construction reveal a structure that resembled a barn that had lost half its roof in a hurricane. The huge space was largely exposed to the elements; it faced south to maximize use of the sun's daily trip across the sky. Long cables to guide the muslin sheets stretched from the rafters to the wall. Inside were wires, lifts, lattices, and Cooper Hewitt lights, the standard for modern filmmaking. When the building was finished, Klutho advertised the space in a California film industry paper. "Enjoy summer this winter" at "this beautiful plant in Jacksonville, Florida." "The finest plant in the South" was "only 30 hours from Broadway." Available to rent or buy.

Save for the low-budget Johnny Ray Players, no one bit on the advertisement, and very quickly Klutho's expensive studio became dead weight. It didn't help that the United States had recently entered World War I and that Klutho's ancestry was German. In only six months, Klutho's studio had gone so far into the red that he began selling precious parcels of real estate he'd been holding in Riverside. For $1,600, buyers could have the lot and free plans for a Klutho-designed home. None sold.[33]

Four years later, in 1921, another attempt was made to revive Jacksonville's struggling film industry, and Klutho was involved in this project as well. At the beginning of World War I, the U.S. military had set up a local training site called Camp Joseph E. Johnson. On New Year's Day 1921, the following was announced in Section Two of the *Florida Times-Union*: "World's Largest Motion Picture Production Center Will Be Built at Camp Jos. E. Johnston." While the city was certainly used to such proclamations, the sheer size of this project peaked interest. According to the article, Fine Arts Pictures, Inc., a New York production headed by Murray Garsson, had purchased Camp Johnston's 700-acre plot as the future site of Fine Arts City, a fully functioning facility where employees would work, live, and entertain. "Where now stand unoccupied barrack buildings and dining halls will rise studios, attractive bungalows for motion picture people, laboratories and other buildings necessary in the operation of this city." The article also mentioned why Jacksonville was chosen by Fine Arts over That Other Film Town: "The Pacific Coast, for long recognized as the home of the motion picture, has become over-run with producing companies."[34]

Working with a budget of $1 million, Fine Arts City would be capable of housing forty different production companies at the same time; plans called for twenty complete motion picture studios, each capable of servicing the

Klutho Studios, one of the last studios built in Jacksonville, included two 50-by-80-foot out-door studios, a retractable roof, prop rooms, dressing rooms, and a projection room. *Florida Photographic Collection, Tallahassee, Florida*

needs of two companies (each of which would get 7,800 square feet of shooting space). A number of permanent sets would be built as well. "Among these will be included typical 'Westerns,' Ghetto streets, a Chinatown section, rural village streets and many others. In addition, a number of large indoor and outdoor swimming pools and diving tanks will be installed." The article emphasized the particular benefits of shooting film in Florida: "Florida far surpasses California in every scenic quality except that of mountains. And mountain scenery of every description is available within twelve hours travel from Jacksonville."[35]

With Richard Garrick's 67,000-square-foot dream complex proving to be nothing more than a complex dream, Garsson turned out to be the voice the local industry desperately needed. "Florida offers the best climactic conditions of any section in the United States for motion picture production," he told the *Florida Times-Union*. He recruited Klutho for the project, who designed the massive complex.[36]

An advertisement for Klutho Studios, which claimed that the studio was the "largest for-rent plant outside New York and West Coast." *Florida Photographic Collection, Tallahassee, Florida*

Within a month of the announcement, trouble was haunting the construction of Fine Arts City. Worried about Garsson's business practices, principal investors in Fine Arts City cut him loose. The investors found a dose of credibility by attaching none other than Hollywood forefather Lewis Selznick to the project. But even with Selznick's influx of cash, the project died on the vine. Cause of death: empty promises, cash shortages, and a board of directors that could not agree about how to move forward. Garsson turned out to be little more than a false prophet. More than twenty years after Fine Arts City's implosion, *Time* published a story that laid out Garsson's prolific history in con artistry.[37] He went to federal prison in 1949 for war profiteering. His *New York Times* obituary in 1957 noted that he died "in poverty" and "was a homeless man at 65."[38]

For Klutho, who was scarred in the Fine Arts debacle, the times ahead would be less than deserving of a man who had led the charge in rebuilding Jacksonville. After years of half-rented spaces, his studio officially closed in 1922. Over the coming decades, his architecture practice slowed to a trickle. On March 4, 1964, Henry John Klutho died due to complications from a stroke. When Klutho passed away, he was near poverty and living in the same Prairie School house he had designed a half-century earlier.[39]

This story should be over. But there was this one other filmmaker who ignored the forecast, ignored the zeitgeist, ignored the racial climate, and walked into an industry in recession. He arrived in Jacksonville after Kalem had left, after Bowden was fired, after the confetti and ticker tape had fallen and been swept up. With the third act nearing the credits, a gentleman originally from North Florida returned home with his family and a strange plan for success: completely ignore the nation's white audiences. While his place in history is hidden in the stacks, his contribution was groundbreaking. Richard Norman, a white man, came home to make black films.

8

Reel People

There is not a white man in the cast, or is there depicted
in the entire picture anything of the usual mimicry of the negro.
—Poster for the film *Green Eyed Monster*

The titles of the black films held at the Library of Congress jump from innocuous to inspiring to incendiary. Under the header "Comedies," you'll find *A Nigger in the Woodpile* and *Who Said Chicken?* Browse over to "Documentaries and Newsreels," and the titles are sour and disconcerting, like aluminum to the tongue: *A Watermelon Contest, Dancing Darkie Boy, Native Women Coaling a Ship and Scrambling for Money.* Elsewhere, one finds groundbreaking films: *Cotton Come to Harlem, A Raisin in the Sun, Sweet Sweetback's Baadasssss Song,* and, naturally, a slew of movies that deconstructed white characters and reconstructed them as black characters (*Blacula, Blackenstein,* and *A Black Sherlock Holmes*). The cast lists of these films and others are a who's who in black cultural history: Cab Calloway, Duke Ellington, Nat King Cole, Spencer Williams, Ossie Davis, Ruby Dee, Sidney Poitier, Melvin Van Peebles, and Harry Belafonte.

About halfway down the alphabetical master list, between two films by Oscar Micheaux (*The Exile* and *The Girl from Chicago*) is *The Flying Ace,*

Richard E. Norman

Richard E. Norman, the director-writer-producer-editor who made black films free of the racial stereotypes typical of the era. *Courtesy: Richard E. Norman Jr.*

directed, written, produced, and edited by Richard E. Norman. His name hardly registers with the more well known names previously mentioned. Neither does anyone in the film's cast: the actors in *The Flying Ace* include little-known lead Laurence Criner and the one-legged wonder Steve "Peg" Reynolds.

But absence of relevance in popular culture doesn't negate why Richard Norman belongs in the Library of Congress, the keeper of our national history (and more than half a million films). He was a filmmaker central to the development of silent black cinema who produced his work in a one-and-a-half-acre film studio in the North Florida suburbs of Jacksonville. He was a white filmmaker who gave black actors a chance to be real. There were no Sambos, Rastuses, Amoses, or Andys. His films starred black heroes, black businessmen, black pilots, black cowboys.

Norman's career in Jacksonville began as the city's film industry was crashing into the rocks. He arrived in a marketplace that one writer described as "beset by tiny margins, cutthroat competition, limited outlets and empty pockets."[1] The Gold Rush was over; the gold rushes, those dailies of car chases down Main Street and St. Johns riverboats belching coal, had died on the cutting-room floor. It was 1921, and everyone had left Jacksonville for somewhere else. Like a flare fired from a sinking ship, Norman's operation signaled the spark of life.

⊰⊱

During the Great Depression, Middleburg, Florida was one of those cities that Farm Security Administration photographers passed through on their way to the next destitute town. They were all over the state, photographing the dry farm fields and empty lumber mills and migrant workers. Gordon Parks was snapping Jim Crow train cars in St. Augustine. Dorothea Lange was in Caryville, shooting unemployed lumber workers stranded in the streets. Marion Post Wolcott found a shaggy-haired boy in Homestead picking tomatoes. "I'm tired and my back hurts, but my mother keeps yellin at me because I'm so slow," the boy told Wolcott. "We come down here in October, mostly because my father used to be a barber but didn't have any work and I needed the sun because I was undernourished and had lung trouble. The doctor in school told them to take me away."[2] The photographers pointed their crosshairs in Pahokee, Palm Beach, Lake Alfred, Lakeland, Sarasota, Sanford, Tampa, Mossy Head, Daytona, Frostproof, Live Oak, and Tarpon Springs. The Library of Congress marks eighty cities the Farm Security Administration visited.

Middleburg, one of the oldest settlements in Florida, was not one of those cities. Even for wide-open Florida, it was, quite literally, a burg in the middle of nowhere. This is where, in 1891, Richard Edward Norman was born. He studied chemistry and the motion picture trade while in college in Tampa, which was growing quite a film community of its own.

Invention, be it stories, chemical recipes, or practical devices, was a constant theme of Norman's life. His earliest business ventures were soft drinks, the first true elixir being Passi Kola: "a concentrated extract of passion flower, kola nut and other tonics, in combination with a delicious flavor for making the finest and most salable soda fountain or bottled beverage ever sold." Norman himself sketched its logo—sweeping, ribbon-like white lettering, quite similar to the logo of another famous soft drink. In the newspaper ad mockup, fruit blossoms flank its promise of "remarkable life-giving power" and the statement that it "restores exhausted nerves, nourishes the brain, adds vigor and strength to the body."[3]

When he shifted gears to film, Norman pioneered quite the niche business: he produced "town films." First as Cameraphone Company of Des Moines, Iowa, and later as Norman Film Manufacturing Company of Chicago, Illinois, Norman traveled to small towns and proposed that he produce a local film: he would cast local actors, use local landmarks as backdrops, and screen the film at the local theater. "The old cut and dried motion picture propositions are dead ones," read the brochure. "They are not making the money. It is the novelties that are real moneymakers as any live exhibitor will concede.

"Have you ever stopped to think of the tremendous drawing power of a good Home Talent comedy photoplay—there is nothing like it for drawing power. It has backed away any high priced star feature off the boards as a money maker and booster for the Theatre man."[4]

A Norman town film went something like this: Norman presented local officials with the brochure and asked them to lend their sons and daughters for the film. Flattered, they spread the word and the wannabes showed up to be cast. The film was shot using the local scenery: churches, views, Main Street, and so forth. Norman would film, develop, and edit the movie at his Iowa headquarters and return the completed version. It would be screened at the local theater, with the profits split 60-40 (the 60 for Norman). The city retained rights and ownership of the film, which Norman pitched as something of a "promotional" film for the city. Mark map. Drive to new town. Repeat.[5]

He covered the Midwest, from Murphysboro, Illinois, to Hannibal, Missouri, to Beloit, Wisconsin, making friends, clients, and stars at every stop. The brochure was filled with "What They've Said" letters from theater owners that were chock-full of superlative praise.

Mr. R. E. Norman made a home talent photoplay that ran for four days in my theatre at an advance admission of 20 cents. The unanimous opinion of my patrons was that it was one of the best pictures ever shown in Oshkosh. It made a big hit with me and my patrons.

CHAS. H CAREY, Mgr. Grand Opera House, Oshkosh, Wis.[6]

While most of the these films were love stories—a couple joyfully wandering through town and ending up at a wedding chapel—Norman also had a stock comedy script the locals could act out. Norman's brochure even listed the props, costumes, and materials necessary to make the comedy: "2 dark slouch hats, one checkered cap, one auto duster and goggles, gunny sack, and local newspaper."[7] This paint-by-numbers script produced the first entry in Norman's oeuvre: *Sleepy Sam the Sleuth.*

The Black Film Center/Archive at Indiana University holds the only copy of this film. Shot in the outer expanses of Des Moines, Iowa (only one telephone pole is counted), it centers on farmer Silas Brown, who discovers that some of his chickens have been stolen. The title cards are filled with corny jokes ("I'll apprehend the fowl criminals," decrees Silas). The title character, Sleepy Sam, is an Inspector Clouseau–like detective who bumbles his way through the investigation and pursuit of justice. It is a physical, farcical romp, with car chases, foot chases, characters who are flattened into cardboard-thin pancakes, and balloon-sized bombs that are tossed back and forth like hot coals. Here's an excerpt from the actual movie script:

Scene No. 46. Chicken thieves running.
Scene No. 47. Italians in pursuit of chicken thieves.
Scene No. 48. Chicken thieves throw bomb at Italians.
Scene No. 49. Bomb passes Italians, knocking them down.
Scene. No. 50. Bomb in air.
Scene No. 51. Bomb in pursuit of Sam.
Scene No. 52. Italians throw two bombs at chicken thieves.
Scene No. 53. Bombs in air.
Scene No. 54. Bombs after chicken thieves.
Scene No. 55. Bomb after Sam.[8]

Norman's next project was the 1916 film *Green Eyed Monster*, a drama centered on two competing railroad companies (the "Green Eyed Monster" was, of course, the almighty dollar). Just like *Sleepy Sam the Sleuth*, *Green Eyed Monster* had an all-white cast (in full disclosure, *Sleepy Sam* had one black character: Willie, a tattered vagabond complete with bandanna knapsack). It was about this time that Norman became familiar with black cinema, with directors such as Oscar Micheaux and producers such as the Lincoln Motion Picture Company. Three years later, after a few missteps and after listening to audience feedback, Norman remade *Green Eyed Monster* with an all-black cast. The response was overwhelmingly positive. The publicity states that the film suggests "advancement of the colored race along educational and financial lines," going on to say it was "even more interesting than the 'usual' thrillers because of the fact that the characters are colored people, splendidly assuming different roles."[9]

The publicity continues, "There is not a white man in the cast, or is there depicted in the entire picture anything of the usual mimicry of the negro. This photo play has been endorsed by the most prominent colored people in America."[10] *Green Eyed Monster* was accepted not only by the general black public (a previously ignored and untapped demographic) but by black critics as well. It was "one of the most spectacular productions ever shown at a local house and has created a furore everywhere it has been exhibited," raved the *Chicago Defender*.[11] Because of the buzz, *Green Eyed Monster* made the full rounds on the black theater circuit: it was screened at the Lincoln Theatre in Baltimore and the Olympia Theatre in East St. Louis, the Paramount in Atlanta and the Apex in Topeka. In February 1921, Norman received a letter from New Orleans producer H. G. Till, who raved about *Green Eyed Monster*, which he had seen at the Temple Theatre. He asked for distribution rights in the South. "It has long been the opinion of the writer that the making of motion pictures with all-negro casts is a money-making branch of this industry that has been too long neglected."[12] The letter underscored Norman's foresight.

Green Eyed Monster marked the turn in Norman's career where the white filmmaker went into business with black heroes.

❄❧

August 15, 1921

Mr. John Owens
P.O. Box 121
Boley, Okla.

Dear Sir:—

The writer had a talk with you some time ago in regard to the prospects of producing a Western Picture in Boley with Colored characters, and you assured him of your co-operation and that you would be able to secure about 20 riders to act for us. . . . The advertising value of a Colored Western Moving Picture Play made in Boley is of tremendous value to your City of Boley as it will bring scenes from your City before thousands of people over the United States. . . . We would like you to take a part in our picture as Sheriff and we can also use the other Sheriff that works with you. . . .

> Yours very truly,
> R. E. Norman[13]

Having done love stories and a railroad thriller, Norman wanted to do a black western. Western? Was there any genre whiter than the western? But Norman had knowledge that black cowboys were an integral part of conquering the West. There was Nat Love, former Tennessee slave and Texas range rover who summed up the cowboy code like no screenwriter ever could: "There is a man's work to be done, and a man's life to be lived, and when death was to be met, he met it like a man."

Norman found a black cowboy in Oklahoma and built a movie around him. His name was Bill Pickett, death-defying rodeo cowboy and star of the Miller Brothers' Wild West Show at the 101 Ranch, an expanse in the all-black town of Boley, Oklahoma. Pickett was a dusty leather-faced roper with a few missing teeth. He was hardly a matinee idol, but his rodeo skills and status as Negro inventor of bulldogging (read "steer wrestling") made him box office gold. Theodore Roosevelt said, "Bill Pickett's name will go down in Western history as being one of the best trained ropers and riders the West ever produced."[14]

The Bull-Dogger was essentially a documentary; its annotation in *Frame by Frame: A Black Filmography* is as follows: "Bill Pickett demonstrates his great skill at 'bull dogging' and other cowboy feats; includes trick riding by black cowboys and cowgirls."[15] But Norman managed to weave a small narrative into the footage and needed a cowgirl to round out the cast. For that role he turned to Anita Bush, known as "the Little Mother of Colored Drama." Norman and Bush had first connected via written correspondence; having heard about his black-cast films, she sent her headshots and résumé. On July 20, 1921, Norman wrote to Bush to invite her to Boley for the film shoot. In his letter, he established his credentials: "In producing *Green Eyed Monster* our 5 reel railroad drama with an all-colored cast, we set a precedent in having a story free from race problems and one full of action with a good moral."[16] Bush accepted the offer and a salary of $30 a week. In her handwritten reply, Bush established her own credentials. She wrote, "My reputation is easily worth that. As I am known in nearly every house in the country. Also white vaudeville and burlesque. As my name is a drawing card in both."[17]

After finding all his extras and getting permission to film at the 101 Ranch, Norman headed to Boley. The extensive footage included Pickett dragging a bull to the ground in a swirling chrysalis of dust; Pickett working the lasso, jumping over, through, and back; riders being knocked out cold and fanned with ten gallon hats; a woman shooting the tip of her cigarette with her pistol and taking a drag of the bullet-lit smoke. Even after cutting *The Bull-Dogger* into "Five Smashing Reels of Thrills! Laughs Too!" there was enough left over for a quasi-sequel. *The Crimson Skull*, featuring Anita Bush, Bill Pickett, and the comedic stylings of Steve Reynolds, "the one-legged wonder," was a "mystery western . . . about outlaws who threaten the peace of law-abiding citizens, and who are bested by the good guys."[18] Years later, Norman made it an Okey trifecta with the release of *Black Gold*, the adventurous autobiographical tale of L. B. Tatums, U.S. marshal and founder of Tatums, Oklahoma, which was the center of the oil boom of the late 1800s.

The Bull-Dogger and *The Crimson Skull* were both hits for Norman. *The Crimson Skull*'s poster called out to theater owners to get in on the action: "Over 6,000 paid admissions in one theatre seating 470. How many colored pictures have you ran that beat that?"[19] The success of these movies allowed Norman to reestablish roots in North Florida. After having had offices in Des Moines, Chicago, and Jacksonville, Norman and his business partner

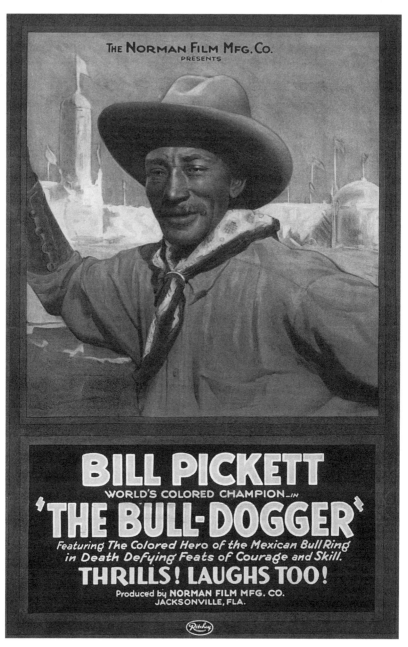

The poster for *The Bull-Dogger*, Richard Norman's western starring rodeo cowboy Bill Pickett, "the colored hero of the Mexican bullring." *Museum of Florida History, Florida Department of State*

and brother Bruce shopped around in 1922 for a facility, a "film plant" that could accommodate their growing operation. The most appealing was the old Eagles Studios, across the St. Johns in Arlington. It was a one-plus-acre plot located at 6337 Arlington Road. Spread across the land were five buildings. The large production building housed a darkroom, a projection room, and a walk-in safe for film storage. There was also an actor's changing cottage, a prop storage garage, and a set building. A swimming pool was set in the middle of the buildings, the pool pump connected to a huge generator. Norman bought the property at a bargain basement price. New letterhead was printed up: the company name was typeset above a picture of the studio, an aerial shot of the white buildings wrapped by ranch-style fencing. It was "the headquarters for information on all Audio Visual Aids," focusing on "talking picture equipment, chemical specialties and motion pictures."[20]

With town films, soft drinks, and white comedies behind him, his professional identity was now set: Norman was the white filmmaker who made black films. But who was Norman? Was he a dedicated racial pioneer or had he simply found a need and filled it? The answer is yes.

Norman the businessman was very practical. He kept impeccable track of his earnings and expenditures. Pieces of scrap paper are filled with line after line of addition, subtraction, and long division. Food, gas, lodging, and car trouble litter his expense reports, which paint the picture of a traveling salesman.

FRIDAY

7 gal. gas.	.52
Toll bridge from Tampa to St. P.	1.58
1 g. oil	.35
Hotel	3.00
Meals	1.90

SATURDAY

Grease for car	4.25
5 gal. gas	1.15
Storage	.50
Hotel	2.00
Meals	2.25

SUNDAY

4 gal. gas	.92
Tow car to Sarasota	3.00
Replace rear joint	12.50
Hotel	2.00
Meals	2.25

Norman the marketer was quite savvy. He was an early proponent of public appearances. The business agreement for a screening of *The Crimson Skull* at the Egypt Theatre in St. Petersburg noted that Norman would provide the film and Steve "Peg" Reynolds in person.[21] In the press sheet for *The Crimson Skull*, Norman suggests ideas to theater owners on how to better sell the film. "Here's another one: decorate your lobby with old guns, saddles and other western curios, boots, etc., hang a card on one of the revolvers reading, 'This is the gun that . . . the mysterious outlaw used in *The Crimson Skull*.' Put out a pair of boots with this card: 'This pair of boots worn by Bill Pickett, world's champion cowboy in *The Crimson Skull*.'"[22] For the 1923 film *Regeneration*, about a couple stranded on a desert island ("the first colored picture with a real sea story and a sex theme"), Norman had a slicker, more scintillating approach. "Here's a tip, Mr. Exhibitor: a 16-year exploitation angle. If you feel that it will stimulate business to bar all children under 16 the picture is strong enough to get by on such a sign, but the theme is handled with all the delicacy so it can be shown to children." He acted as both the Motion Picture Association of America and its violator.[23]

Today, Norman the filmmaker would be considered an independent. And although he worked in something of a controversial genre, Norman's cinematic tastes leaned toward the modern blockbuster. He liked action, he liked drama, he liked mystery, he liked comedy, and he liked them as ingredients in the same pot. Take for example the movie poster for the 1926 picture *The Flying Ace*. The words *Love! Laughs! Mystery!* arc across the placard. In his town film brochure, Norman suggested that the locals write their own scripts and gave them hints about what made for successful content: "A plot not too brazenly cinematic, but natural enough to lead the audience along, is melodramatic enough to please those who want thrills, romantic enough to satisfy the seeker of the emotional, and contains room for action enough to put the film across."[24]

Norman was not afraid to titillate with his films. In 1924, the State of

The poster for *The Flying Ace*, the black-cast film Richard Norman dubbed "the greatest airplane mystery thriller ever produced." *Florida Photographic Collection, Tallahassee, Florida*

New York Motion Picture Commission reviewed *Regeneration* and asked for an edit. "Reel #2: Shorten scene one half—struggle between the crew and Captain on the stern of boat and eliminate scene of the girl (Olive) with pistol holding up the crew." The reason for the elimination: "tend[s] to incite crime."[25]

But there was more than entertainment on the line here, and Norman knew it. According to Richard Norman Jr., the filmmaker's son, "My dad, of course, was a businessman. But an underlined thought in his mind was the desire to do something constructive to better race relations. Through his films he was committed to helping black players live up to their potential and show what they were capable of as performers and human beings."[26] He was very generous to his stable of actors and crew. They lived in the Arlington studio's residential quarters during filming and were often invited to the Norman home for holiday dinners. Thanksgivings were always very busy.

Norman had in part put the black film industry on his shoulders, and his films became emblematic of that industry's progress. But he was in a tricky position. Any misstep he made would be carried by an entire race, not just by him alone. In June 1923, Norman wrote to Clarence Brooks, a black producer in Los Angeles, asking Brooks to come to Jacksonville and partner up on a fifteen-reel black serial titled *Zircon*. "I have personally interviewed every theatre owner and have played every theatre catering to a colored audience and it is no secret among colored theatre owners that some of our pictures to-day hold records that . . . have not been broken by any other colored picture." Norman called the *Zircon* project "risky" but was steadfast in his professional opinion. "If the colored theatre owner don't want a serial, we won't cram it down his throat—but he does want one."[27] Brooks wrote back two weeks later, confessing to "have given favorable consideration" to *Zircon* and being "deeply interested in the future of the Negro on the screen." Brooks wrote that a good black film needed four fundamentals: "good story, good actors, a good production—with good exploitation angles." Brooks noted that anything else "will do more to hinder the progress and popularity of colored pictures than all of the efforts put forth heretofore." Although Brooks passed on the project, he wished Norman well, signing off the letter, "Yours for the success of colored pictures, Clarence A. Brooks."[28]

Norman the distributor was very effective. He sold his own films and those of others by tapping into a network of black film exchanges and exhibitors. In the summer of 1926, none other than Oscar Micheaux contacted Norman about screening *Regeneration* at the Franklin Theatre in New York City. Micheaux was rather blunt in his letter to Norman. Perhaps Micheaux saw something simpatico in this producer, just two outlaw auteurs riding saddle to saddle, fighting for black cinema together. At one point, Micheaux critiqued other black films on the market. "Some Jews have produced a couple of features, the first of which appears to draw very well although mighty badly acted and poorly photographed."[29]

Taboo topics were a common sell for Norman. He had a particular interest in convict and prison films. In the spring of 1923, Norman contacted Western Feature Films of Chicago about rights to the "five reel super-special prison picture" *Death in the Electric Chair*. Produced with the permission of Sing Sing Prison, *Death in the Electric Chair* showed "with gruesome realism the whipping post, the damp and durky [*sic*] dungeons, the horrors of the death chamber, the brutality of capital punishment."[30] For lobby decor, Western Feature Films offered a replica of the Sing Sing electric chair. Norman also screened the Selig-produced *Who Shall Take My Life*? "six reels of the greatest prison photo-drama ever made." The Selig press sheet described it as "a soul stirring play to abolish capital punishment. Interwoven in the play is a plot of enduring love and undying hate."[31]

Norman the romantic was no slouch either. He met his wife Gloria in Marionette, Wisconsin, likely a stop on his town film tour. When they met, Norman dropped a young line that would become one of the oldest in the book. Gloria Norman relayed the story to a *Florida Times-Union* reporter in 1975. "I'm sure you know the line. He asked me if I'd like to be in movies, and I said sure."[32]

Her first film: *The Wrecker*. Next: *Marionette Adopts a Baby*. When the couple moved into the Arlington studio, Gloria opened a dance studio in the production building.

¾ ¾

Zircon, Norman's ambitious fifteen-reel serial, was never made. But one episode had been written. It was "The Sky Demon," an aviation adventure starring colored pilots. It was this idea that would get Norman into the Library of Congress.

"The Sky Demon" was inspired in part by Bessie Coleman, "the only colored aviator in the world." Her live air shows were popular in both America and Europe, and her representatives contacted Norman about making a film about her life. Coleman's biopic was titled *Yesterday, Today and Tomorrow*.

Coleman's representative, D. Ireland Thomas, manager of the Lincoln Theatre in Charleston, South Carolina, wrote to Norman in January 1926. "She desires to have a production made of her self and I am thinking that you might work out a plan to use her in a production with a story built around her and her plane. . . . I think it would be a winner."[33] Norman replied two weeks later, intrigued by the idea. "There is no doubt," wrote Norman, "that with a picture of five or six reels, properly acted and full of action with [Bessie Coleman] in the leading role, would be a good drawing card in the colored theatres."[34] Unfortunately, Coleman died in an airplane crash before the project materialized.

The idea stayed with Norman. And why not? An airplane thriller had all the adrenalin required of a Norman picture. He wrote a script that would be "the greatest airplane mystery thriller ever produced." On the script's cover sheet: *The Flying Ace*.

The story revolves around Billy Stokes, a pilot, war hero, and former railroad detective. Coincidentally, just as Stokes's plane lands back in his hometown, three thieves accost the local railroad manager and steal $25,000 from the payroll. The cast features Laurence Criner as Billy Stokes; Kathryn Boyd as Ruth, Stokes's love interest and the daughter of the railroad manager; and the ever-reliable Steve "Peg" Reynolds as Criner's sidekick and comic relief. Early in the film, Reynolds strums his cane like a guitar and sings, "I don't bother work, work don't bother me / I'se for times happy as a bumblebee."

The film was released in 1926, the same year as James Cruze's classic *Old Ironsides*, which pitted an American fighting ship against Barbary pirates. *The Flying Ace* was the ultimate hybrid action flick: fistfights, dogfights, chases on bicycles and in horse-drawn carriages, and cameo appearances by all of the seven deadly sins. And in marketing *The Flying Ace*, Norman laced the film's backstory with heavy doses of hype and outright fabrication. The press sheet reads, "Realizing the impossibility of securing competent colored players who could really fly, they set about constructing a special plane which could be operated by inexperienced flyers." The plane "was constructed true to scale and patterned exactly after the famous Curtiss J.N.D.4s. It was powered with a Ford motor with electrical starter." Yet the press sheet adds that the "cool headed" actors were dealing with "an engine of death." The truth was that all the pilots stayed on the ground in the yard at Norman's studio. Some strategically blown neck scarves gave the shots all the authenticity they needed.[35]

"Mama, darlin," if I'm a success in this show, well, we're gonna move from here. Oh yes, we're gonna move up to the Bronx. A lot of nice green grass up there and a whole lot of people you know. . . . And I'm gonna buy you a nice black silk dress, Mama. . . . and I'm gonna get you a nice pink dress that'll go with brown eyes."

When that sixteen-inch wax disc first yammered Al Jolson's lines to America's film audiences, that was it. The "talkie" officially arrived, and the impact left a grim, well, silence. How ironic is it that 1927's *The Jazz Singer*, a musical in which the white star wears blackface, was the picture that grounded Norman's career.

By 1929, Norman's films were known worldwide. That year, he received a letter from a motion picture company in Liberia. "We are anxious to introduce Negro Artists into our shows here in Liberia, a thing that has never been heretofore, we respectfully request that you send us at your very earliest convenience a full list with prices of your old and latest films."[36] The problem was that Norman's actors were mute, their lips moving for the sake of movement, and "talkies" were exploding nationwide. In 1929, sound equipment was being installed in 250 theaters each month.[37] Because of sound, film audiences swelled from 60 million in 1927 to 110 million in 1929. As a result of this boom, "the hundred-per-cent talkie became recognized as the established form for all future productions."[38]

Norman the inventor had had his eye on voice synchronization for some time. When the Depression bore down and finances became tight, he went all in, pouring his entire savings into building voice synchronization equipment. The result was a spindly contraption that resembled a chemist's laboratory balanced on a carpenter's horse. A tube connected the camera to the nearby phonograph recorder with a twelve-inch wax record. The Camera Phone worked, and it worked well. All of a sudden, there were new business cards in Arlington offering "talking picture equipment and supplies." A form letter to filmmakers followed. "Now you can secure a small, portable Talking Picture Unit that is dependable and one you are sure of SUCCESS with," the letter read. "You know the first class road-man is too busy to be fussing with apparatus that must be nursed along and requires from 10 to 28 connections of a hay wire nature."[39]

They were priced at $6,000 a pop, and at first they sold quite well.[40] But then Western Electric, which years earlier had sued Alexander Graham Bell over patent rights to the telephone, had its own idea. While Warner Brothers technology made *The Jazz Singer* possible, their sound recording machine was a cumbersome contraption. The answer was bringing the technology in-

side the projector. To do so, the sound recording was quarantined to a skinny
strip that ran lengthwise along the film stock. Western Electric developed
a 35-millimeter projector that ate the strip's code and regurgitated it as an
actor's monologue or Al Jolson's hammy voice. The sound was then fed to a
gramophone-like horn at the front of the theater. Western Union's creation
became standard; Norman's became obsolete. Bankruptcy followed.

At one point after Norman's fall, Warner Brothers offered Norman a job.
He declined. He chose to hold on to Norman Studios—his home, his identity—and produce industrial films for companies like Pure Oil. As Norman's
film business went dry, the buildings were put to other uses. Eventually Gloria Norman's dance studio took over the production building, where it stayed
for thirty years.

The Industry Moves On

Despite very crude and unpleasant handicaps
picture makers have repeatedly gone to Florida.
—D. W. Griffith

Real estate developers Woodruff and Shoults contacted the Crescent Sign Company in 1923. The duo wanted a huge sign to promote their new residential development, advertised as "a superb environment on the Hollywood side of the hills." The Crescent Sign Company's owner, Thomas Goff, designed it himself: 13 letters, each letter 50 feet high by 30 feet wide, embedded with electric lights.

HOLLYWOODLAND.

The beaming white sign was placed near the summit of Mount Lee, a hillside of sun-bleached rocks and pepper trees overlooking Beachwood Canyon—a set of porcelain veneers amidst a teenager's pocked complexion. The sign was only meant to be temporary, up long enough to sell the necessary parcels. But it became so popular that it never came down; in fact, it was adopted by the city and underwent routine facelifts. In 1949, the Hollywood Chamber of Commerce offered some repairs. As part of the renovation, the last four letters were removed.

HOLLYWOOD.

The sign became more than a city's trademark. It became an industry's trademark. High up on a hill, protected by chain-link fence and a security system, the Hollywood sign is that unattainable something. It is the lighthouse for big-screen dreams. It's the big white metaphor for Making It.

For Jacksonville, the sign was a gravestone. It marked the death of Hollywood's first and only competition. The deceased was a turn-of-the-century East Coast film town that once drew industry elites and wide-eyed hucksters. As the city imploded from a combination of greed, war, an epidemic, and changing morals, the West Coast raised its nine iconic letters and toasted a new and future monopoly.

We know what went wrong for Jacksonville. But what did Hollywood and Los Angeles do right? While much of it has to do with logistics, trends, and politics, much was also coincidental. Hollywood had the benefit of being a blank economic slate when the industry arrived. By comparison, Jacksonville was already crowded with industry when Kalem hit town. There was shipping, agriculture, and tourism. Los Angeles had its groves but was largely empty, the kind of place an industry could commandeer. It became a place where talent could start fresh. A place where actors could lose their baggage, cultural heritage, and ethnic names. It is this town where Gloria Svensson became Gloria Swanson, Frederick Austerlitz became Fred Astaire, Julius Ullman became Douglas Fairbanks, Margarita Cansino became Rita Hayworth, and Asa Yoelson became Al Jolson.

The allure of starting over appealed to the huddled masses of the attractive and ordinary. In *Movie Made America*, Robert Sklar describes the Hollywood scene of the 1920s, which is eerily similar to today. "Actors and actresses could be and were discovered clerking in drugstores. . . . There were compensations if you kept yourself slim, tanned, well-groomed and -dressed, if your bearing was sure and your manner dynamic. . . . They were a new race, these men and women of the movies. . . . They were a people dedicated more completely to the body, to beauty and health, than any the world had seen before."[1]

This mad, desperate rush gave Hollywood endless fuel for its enduring reputation: the dark, sinful chasm of mystery and intrigue. It's a reputation that birthed its own industry: celebrity tabloid publishing. "A manual of perspective movie players claimed in the mid-1920s that some five thousand persons, mainly young and innocent women, disappeared from sight every year in Hollywood. There were tales of nice Midwestern girls who ended up in brothels and opium dens."[2] Proving, or perhaps establishing, that any publicity is good publicity, Hollywood players were constantly in newspaper stories about depression and failure, murder and suicide. How could one ignore the 1921 headline, "Actress Dies at Drunken Party; Famous Movie Comedian Charged with Murder"? Comedic actor Fatty Arbuckle was having a party at a San Francisco hotel when one of the guests, Virginia Rappe, went into the bedroom to lie down. She was later found half-dressed and dead. Arbuckle was tried three times for murder and manslaughter; the first two juries were hung, the third found him innocent. He was more famous than ever, but his career was ruined. A year later, director William Desmond Taylor was found murdered in his Hollywood home. It was a story that involved cheating husbands and jealous wives, and it was consumed by the tabloids like chum in a shark tank. And in 1932, a troubled young actress named Peg Entwistle jumped to her death from the Hollywood sign's giant "H."

But there was more than just tragedy happening in these hills. It was a crowded factory churning out popular entertainment. LA was a dense constellation of star power—Aries with billboard advertisements—where one mogul neighbored the next and the next. Jack, Sam, and Albert Warner had established their studio on Sunset Boulevard. Nearby was Jesse Lasky's studio, one block from Hollywood and Vine. William Selig's production headquarters was a 32-acre plot near Lincoln Park. Only part of it was an actual studio; the rest was home to the animals used in Selig's films. Louis B. Mayer, the former New England theater owner, moved to Los Angeles to become a movie producer. By the late 1910s, Mayer was renting part of Selig's compound: four stages plus offices, dressing rooms, and bungalows for the talent.[3] Thanks to his eponymous production company and Metro Pictures, which he formed with Richard Rowland in 1915, Mayer's legacy is that he provided the bookend "M's" for current powerhouse MGM. And these moguls were not just making movies, they were making money hand over fist. Around 1914, Thomas Ince was the first movie mogul to build a mansion in the new district known as Beverly Hills.

Jacksonville offered none of Hollywood's intrigue. It was practical—direct rail access from New York!—but not sexy or dangerous. With the movie theaters closing one by one, and Mayor John Martin's administration treating film as a vice, the city drifted into obscurity.

But Jacksonville's rise and fall did have an influence; Jacksonville disseminated the industry to others places within the state. What Jacksonville started would be carried on by other cities like Tampa, Miami, Sarasota, and

Orlando. These places turned supporting roles into starring roles, while Jacksonville licked its wounds and held on to history. From the 1920s through the 1970s, Jacksonville would watch the film and entertainment industry flourish everywhere except the place that first gave it a home.

꒰ ꒱

The Other West Coast

Tampa has the kind of seedy history that makes for good content. The city's football team, the Tampa Bay Buccaneers, is named after a Caribbean pirate, after all. It is a town of immigrants where Sicilians, Cubans, and Spaniards ran their rackets. Soon, organized crime became Tampa's primary trade. Starting in the 1920s, the mob had as great a presence here as it did in New York.

Much of the city's allure was its geographic location. Tampa Bay was a labyrinth of hidden inlets, waterways, and coves, ideal for moving molasses and other raw ingredients for the production of illicit alcohol during Prohibition. In fact, the city, tucked away from the Gulf of Mexico behind dangling peninsulas and waterways, is like the crime boss at a back table of the Tropicana: you'll have to bob and weave through countless obstacles before finally meeting face to face.

The real boss of Tampa was Santo Trafficante Sr. The Mafia don came to dominance in the 1930s, running rackets and other illegal operations. His son, Santo Trafficante Jr., took the family business even further. During the 1940s and 1950s, Junior's fingers were dipped into pies from Tampa Bay to the Bay of Pigs—bolita lotteries in Ybor City, casinos at the Sevilla Biltmore and the Riviera in Havana, and hush-hush handshakes with the Gambino and Genovese families of New York.

In the midst of all this, film sneaked in and began making its name. The first big coup came thanks to local advertising executive Trenton Collins, who in 1931 helped the Committee for the Development of Motion Picture Industry revive film work in the Sunshine State. A year later, Governor Doyle Carlton established a state-funded advisory group for the committee. In 1933, as part of the state's support of the film industry, the legislature authorized a fifteen-year exemption from state and local property taxes. The law eliminated a significant cost for production companies looking to buy large parcels of land or massive ready-made warehouses.[4]

At about that same time, Tampa made news for producing Florida's first talkie. It was the 1930 film *Hell Harbor*, about a young woman who escapes

The poster for *Hell Harbor*, the first "talkie" produced in Florida. The film, starring Lupe Velez, was shot in Tampa. *Collection of the Museum of Florida History, Florida Department of State*

the boredom of island life by heading to Havana. The film starred Lupe Velez, the Mexican-born beauty largely typecast in Latin American roles. She was especially popular as Carmelita Lindsay in the *Mexican Spitfire* series. From 1940 to 1943, she starred in *Mexican Spitfire, Mexican Spitfire Out West, Mexican Spitfire Sees a Ghost, Mexican Spitfire's Elephant,* and *Mexican Spitfire's Blessed Event,* where Carmelita's boyfriend Dennis mistakenly thinks the big impending event is the arrival of Carmelita's baby when in fact the event is her cat's new litter of kittens.

In 1933, the local industry got its own blessed event with the arrival of Buster Keaton. The Great Stone Face was looking for a comeback and was lured to nearby St. Petersburg by Aubrey Kennedy, the producer who made *The Yellow Menace* in Jacksonville in 1916 (a xenophobic look at Asian influence on the white man). Keaton moved to St. Pete and formed his own production firm: the Flamingo Film Company. But "the former silent star became so appalled by the summer heat and insect swarms that he aborted the entire project."[5] A statewide land bust in 1926 and the failure of studio projects like Sun City and Studio Park subsequently shut down any big hopes. From that point forward, Tampa's dangerous and sexy stars would be guys with names like Santo, Vinnie, Jimmy, Jo-Jo, and Mario, and their stories wouldn't be told by screenwriters but the Federal Bureau of Investigations and the Florida Supreme Court.

Movie Magic in the Magic City

For much of the late eighteenth century, Miami was a wild, wild south where few ventured; the first residents of the area were Tequesta Indians, who lived, fought and died in the Key Biscayne shallows. In Patrick D. Smith's *A Land Remembered,* arguably the most enduring work of Florida fiction, the author uses protagonist and third-generation Floridian Sol MacIvey to articulate just where Miami had came from. "You can't go anywhere without stepping on the skull of some man or animal that was killed," Sol tells the driver of his Roll Royce as it crosses MacArthur Causeway. "The whole damned place is littered with bones."[6]

But Henry Flagler's railroad helped change that after the turn of the century. The masses followed the tracks south until they reached Miami and ultimately Key West. By 1915 the Greater Miami Chamber of Commerce and its six-time president Everest Sewell were buying space in northern magazines to advertise Miami as a winter destination. In no time at all Miami was a tropigapolis, a heavily populated city 500 miles farther south than Los Angeles. Business was booming and there were lots of hotels and paved roads to accommodate tourism. Oh, the tourism. Miami was the main reason that everyone recognized those famous 1940s "Greetings from Florida" postcards with the big block letters. A sailboat in the "O," a hibiscus in the "R," flamingoes in the "A."

The film industry came in small waves, but two people made Miami an entertainment force to be reckoned with. The first was D. W. Griffith, who came to Florida after collecting the earnings from his racist epic *The Birth of a Nation*. By 1919, Griffith's private corporation held more than $3.4 million. That year, Griffith "decamped with most of his company to Fort Lauderdale. Besides its calming effect on his emotional life, there were other advantages to be found in the South. He hated working in the cold, he loved exploring new locations."[7]

Setting up shop along the New River, where today there is a riverwalk with New Orleans–themed restaurants, surf shops, and rock clubs, Griffith's production company created a stir in South Florida. The locals were both voyeurs (decamping to watch the on-set action) and volunteers (Seminole Indians were cast as extras).[8]

The only problem was that Griffith's Florida output was some of the least thrilling and most cursed of his career. The first was the 1920 film *The Idol Dancer*, starring Richard Barthelmess (later nominated for an Academy Award for *The Patent Leather Kid*) and Clarine Seymour. Sadly, *The Idol Dancer* was Seymour's twentieth and final film. While shooting a scene in a coconut grove near Las Olas Boulevard, Seymour fell out of a coconut tree. She completed the film but died afterward from a twisted intestine. Others troubles arose as well. The film crew, including Griffith and his lead actors, got lost on their way to Nassau, Bahamas, where they planned to shoot some additional scenes. Navy and Coast Guard ships found them on a deserted island three days later.[9]

The trouble and tragedy didn't deter Griffith. His faith in South Florida filmmaking remained—for the moment. The filmmaker produced *The Love Flower*, a story of passion and murder in the South Seas, the same year as *The Idol Dancer*. But he became exasperated by the lack of adequate production

D. W. Griffith (*seated*), legendary director of *The Birth of a Nation*, made films in South Florida during the 1920s. Billy Bitzer (*behind camera*) was Griffith's longtime cinematographer. *Florida Photographic Collection, Tallahassee, Florida*

facilities. On July 11, 1921, Griffith wrote a letter to Everest Sewell and his colleague E. R. Brackett at the Greater Miami Chamber of Commerce after hearing rumors of a possible film studio being built:

> We understand you are about to establish a motion picture studio near Miami, Florida. Certainly Florida needs one. The lack of studio facilities must necessarily discourage many producers in their plans to go there for work. Florida has a great many advantages in picture making, but primitive conditions there compared to the very modern facilities in California argues against Florida. Despite very crude and unpleasant handicaps picture makers have repeatedly gone to Florida, and we believe their visits would be materially increased, were there adequate and reasonable studio facilities.[10]

Griffith's third Florida feature is interesting not only because of location but also because of storyline. While making his other films, Griffith collected "a number of newsclippings dealing with the transgressions—mainly sexual—of clergymen. . . . 'Pastor Father of Child of 17-Year-Old Girl, Jury Decides and He Is Jailed.' . . . 'Suicide of Woman Causes Wife to Sue Minister For Divorce.' . . . 'The Rev. Henry Brockman, Lutheran minister, under arrest for white slavery, shot himself in Iron River, Michigan.'"[11] That fascination manifested itself in his 1923 film *The White Rose*, the story of Joseph Beaugarde, a young pastor who meets orphan Bessie "Teazie" Williams. He gets her pregnant and, racked with guilt, leaves her to return to his ministry. The abandoned and pregnant Bessie is taken in by a black family. After the bastard child is born, Bessie seeks out her Bible-thumping lover, who sees his offspring in the flesh and has a change of heart. He ditches his fiancé and marries Bessie instead. In great contrast to *The Birth of a Nation*, here the blacks are earnest and helpful, upright and pure. But ideological improvement made little difference—*The White Rose* did not meet the artistic or commercial high-water mark of *The Birth of a Nation*. Griffith soon left Florida, shifting his focus to United Artists, the Hollywood production company he founded in 1919 with Charlie Chaplin, Douglas Fairbanks, and Mary Pickford, all of whom were firmly rooted on the West Coast.

Legendary animator and cartoonist Max Fleischer was another big shot who heard about the Florida tax incentives. Fleischer and his family had emigrated from Krakow, Poland, in 1887, settling in the Brownsville section of Brooklyn. He began his career at the *Brooklyn Daily Eagle*, earning $2 a week

D. W. GRIFFITH

❀ SECOND ANNUAL NEW YORK SEASON ❀
FORTY-FOURTH STREET THEATRE

GENERAL OFFICES: 303 LONGACRE BUILDING
TELEPHONE, BRYANT 6761, 6762, 9486
ALBERT L. GREY, GENERAL MANAGER

July 11, 1921

My dear Messrs. Sewell and Brackett:----

We understand you are about to establish a
motion picture studio near Miami, Florida.

Certainly Florida needs one. The lack of
studio facilities must necessarily discourage many producers
in their plans to go there for work.

Florida has a great many advantages in
picture making, but primitive conditions there compared to
the very modern facilities in California argue against
Florida.

Despite very crude and unpleasant handicaps
picture makers have repeatedly gone to Florida, and we
believe their visits would be materially increased, were
there adequate and reasonable studio facilities.

Sincerely,

DWGriffith

Mr. E. G. Sewell,
President Miami Chamber of Commerce
and
Mr. E. R. Brackett.

D. W. GRIFFITH INCORPORATED Presents
"WAY DOWN EAST"

A letter from D. W. Griffith to the Miami Chamber of Commerce complaining
that Florida's production facilities were "primitive" compared to those in California.
Florida Photographic Collection, Tallahassee, Florida

as the art department's errand boy. He landed a job as staff cartoonist, only to leave and establish his own business. Max and his brother Dave ran Fleischer Studios from a small flat at 1600 Broadway.

In the late 1920s, Paramount announced its news series *Talkartoons*. One trade paper advertisement declared, "Paramount *Talkartoons* are something entirely new and entirely different from anything ever seen and heard before. For the first time cartoons will be actually talking pictures." Fleischer had seen his popular character Ko-Ko the Clown upstaged in the public arena by a fusion of ink-black spheres called Mickey Mouse. He got in with Paramount in the hope of creating something even bigger. In 1930, Fleischer created the animated short *Dizzy Dishes*, featuring a canine female that "was nameless, but what a character it was—gross, ugly with an enormous, bouncy behind. However, it did have round, saucer-like eyes and shapely feminine legs."[12]

Paramount went nuts for the zoomorphic bombshell. In subsequent films, she began to look more feminine, trading snout for nose, bulbous waist for big bosom. Her name was Betty Boop, the sassy flapper, the animated sex symbol of the Jazz Age.

Suddenly, Fleischer Studios was the house that Betty Boop built. "Merchandising took off with Betty Boop dolls, clothes, dishes, fan clubs, you name it. The character had her own daily comic strip and a Sunday strip as well. The Bamberger Broadcasting System carried a weekly fifteen-minute coast-to-coast Betty Boop radio show called *Betty Boop Fables*."[13]

The Fleischer empire continued with more hits. He made Superman into an animated series for Paramount and was paid a handsome $100,000 per reel.[14] The high rate proved worthwhile: the first short in the series, simply titled *Superman*, was nominated for an Academy Award. He also sketched the squinting sailor with cantaloupe forearms named Popeye the Sailor. For a time, Fleischer and Walt Disney were competing for the name of top animation studio in the world.

A bitter labor strike in New York got Fleischer thinking about a move somewhere else. But he loved New York. He even looked New York. With his portly stomach, slicked-back hair, and dense moustache, Max could have been the original model for the baker on every New York pizza box. The Fleischers also loved Miami Beach; they had vacationed there several times. He bought a winter home in Miami Beach in 1933, a Spanish-style residence on Alton Road. A few years later, with Paramount's blessing (and financial backing), Fleischer Studios began construction on a new animation studio. It was a one-story concrete fortress on the corner of Northwest 13th Avenue and 17th Street in Miami. In his book *Out of the Inkwell*, Max's son David Fleischer describes the facility: "The new studio was the first completely air-conditioned building in Florida. Its sound-recording stage and mixing equipment were state-of-the-art, as were its fifty-seat theater and projection system. Every detail, from the cafeteria to the machine shop, was impeccably designed and built."[15] Fleischer benefited from the fifteen-year tax exemption but had to sue the state of Florida to get it.

By 1941, Fleischer Studios had completed two features: *Gulliver's Travels* and *Mr. Bug Goes to Town*. Just as the studio was ramping up for its next success, it all came crashing down. On May 29 of that year, a 65-page contract arrived in Miami from Paramount Studios. It noted that not only was the partnership over but that Fleischer Studios had to immediately pay back all funds used to build the studio. The amortization loan agreement had disappeared. It was studio strong-arming at its finest. But the worst of it was that Paramount seized control of all of the studio's creative property: Ko-Ko, Popeye, Betty Boop, the entire stable of characters. Fleischer Studios moved back to New York, back to 1600 Broadway, and sued Paramount to no avail.[16] Today, ownership of Fleischer's work is scattered, gobbled up by the major studios: CBS Paramount handles television distribution, Lions Gate Home Entertainment holds home video rights, Time Warner owns the *Popeye* series, and King Features Syndicate, part of the Hearst Corporation, claims Betty Boop.

There's a Mouse in the House

In 1928, the Walt Disney Company produced *Steamboat Willie, The Gallopin' Gaucho*, and *Plane Crazy*, thereby making Mickey Mouse a megastar. The roughly three decades that followed cemented the company's legend. Between 1928 and 1960, Disney produced Snow White and the Seven Dwarfs (the studio's first animated feature), Goofy, Pluto, Donald Duck, *Silly Symphonies, Sleeping Beauty, Fantasia, Cinderella*, and the Oscar-winning *Pinocchio*. This string of success didn't just tap into our appetite for cutesy, cuddly creatures; for a family entertainment mogul, Disney sure had a knack for embracing subversive, surreal villains. Disney animation has employed Medusa, the Headless Horseman, and Hades, Greek god of the dead. Consider *Peter Pan*'s Captain Hook. The one-handed buccaneer with a bulbous nose and moustache resembling dueling hypodermic needles calls to mind Salvador Dalí, the very epitome of subversive and surreal (Dalí actually worked on an animated film for Disney titled *Destino*). Maybe that was another of Fleischer's problems: a character stable without any good bad guys. Thanks to that and other circumstances, Disney lost its closest competition.

Disney had also built a hugely successful theme park in Anaheim, California, just north of Los Angeles. By 1963, Disney was prepping its sequel: a bigger and better theme part east of the Mississippi. The hush-hush plan was known internally as "Project X," and Disney brass had been scouting sites since 1959. But the right spot proved difficult to find. Among the contenders were Niagara Falls (with parcels on both sides of the U.S.-Canada border), the Baltimore-Washington area, and St. Louis. Disney liked St. Louis the most; the Mississippi riverfront inspired countless ideas for attractions: riverboats, ferries, riverwalks, quaint Rockwellian town squares. Disney was ready to make the deal, but at an eleventh-hour dinner party, everything went wrong. The soiree included politicos, businessmen, and entrepreneurs. Among them was August Busch Jr., head of the Anheuser-Busch megabrewery. One of the evening's talking points was the selling of liquor in the park. Family-oriented Disney would have none of it. But Busch, perhaps full of his namesake lubricant, shared another opinion. "Any man who thinks he can design an attraction that is going to be a success in this city and not serve beer or liquor, ought to have his head examined." What followed was an audible silence. Just like that, the deal was off the table.[17]

Project X was back at square one. Niagara Falls and Baltimore-Washington were off the list—who wanted to be at a theme park in twenty-degree weather? Some Mid-Atlantic states were considered in passing. Then Florida entered the picture. Ocala, with its ranches and green expanses, was an early contender, but access was an issue. Disney's scope was hundreds of thousands of people in and out, and the area's tiny dirt roads and one-lane thoroughfares weren't even close to the infrastructure he needed.

Orlando, some 70 miles southeast of Ocala, was next. A private plane ride was scheduled for an aerial look at the area. Walt looked out the window. "That's it," he said.[18]

Drive through Central Florida today, and you get a glimpse of what Disney was looking at in 1963. Take I-4 west from Kissimmee or pick a direction on John Young Parkway and you'll see loads of untouched land. It's Florida much like it was in the earliest pages of Smith's *A Land Remembered*. There are wide swaths of sawgrass and swamp, and long winding rivulets that empty into the horizon. And this land remembered goes on and on. It's the kind of unending space that's either left to its own devices or becomes home to those blighted structures society banishes to the edges of town. Take SR-528 West from the Space Coast, a thirty-mile stretch of evergreen thicket, and you'll see only two structures: a maximum security prison and a coal-fired power plant.

Disney's eyes caught a younger version of that scene. Out his plane window he saw "a vast stretch of virgin land, much of it swampy and alligator-infested. . . . To the east was McCoy Jet Airport, a hybrid military-civilian base that would later metamorphose into Orlando International Airport." But there was something besides space that Disney saw on that ride: connectivity. Under construction that year was I-4 and the Florida Turnpike. At a press conference in 1965, Disney was asked what drew him to Orlando. "The freeway routes, they bisect here," he said matter-of-factly. Which was quite true—these highways connected to one-lane roads as well as huge interstates. It all equaled the clean movement of tourists. In his book *Married to the Mouse*, Richard Fogelsong writes, "I-4 connects with I-95, which runs up the Atlantic coast from Key West to Maine, and . . . Florida's Turnpike links via I-75 with I-10, which spans the country from the Florida panhandle to California. Whether tourists were driving south from New Jersey or east across Mississippi and Alabama, Orlando was well located—just what Disney consultants wanted."[19]

Project X was to be much grander than what they'd created in Anaheim—the Matterhorn was a good attraction, for starters. This was to be a "total destination resort," a park ten times the size of Disneyland with rides, restaurants, hotels, its own transportation system, and a domed biosphere town called the City of Tomorrow (later the Experimental Prototype Community of Tomorrow, popularly known as EPCOT). In 1965, after much negotiation, the Orlando land purchases were finalized. Disney made forty-seven separate purchases of land totaling 27,258 acres. The cost: just over $5 million.[20]

In May of that year, the *Orlando Evening Star* (later the *Orlando Sentinel*) ran an editorial titled "Mystery Buy Tops $5M." There was much speculation about who the buyer was, Disney being a frontrunner, but the writer urged restraint. "The land buyer would not hesitate to pull out and leave a $5-million real estate investment." The writer was right; St. Louis had learned that lesson the hard way.[21] By the fall, speculation was about to trump truth. To avoid letting his project descend into tabloid, Disney made it official. On the morning of October 29, locals awoke to a newspaper carrying a big banner headline: "It's Official: This Is Disneyland."[22]

In 1976, the *New York Times* laid out what Disney had spent on the project. The figure was approximately $600 million: $100 million for the amusement park, $75 million for EPCOT, and $10 million to $15 million annually for upgrades and upkeep.[23] In 1967, Florida governor Claude Kirk laid out what the world would spend on Disney World: an estimated $3.9 billion in tourist dollars. In addition, the state anticipated $2.2 billion from new job income and more than $400 million for the purchase of construction equipment.[24]

Disney World's grand opening in 1971 was the unveiling of an entertainment Eden. Tourists became loyalists became permanent residents. "Between Disney's opening in 1971 and 1999, Orange County's population more than doubled, swelling from 344,000 to 846,000 residents. . . . And its hotel room count exploded from 8,000 before Disney World to over 100,000 by 2000."[25]

But the megapark's relationship with Orlando was touchy. Author Richard Fogelsong describes Disney World as a "private government, a sort of Vatican with mouse ears. . . . The entertainment titan was authorized . . . to regulate land use, provide fire and police services, build roads, lay sewer lines, license the manufacture and sale of alcoholic beverages, even to build an airport and nuclear power plant." These were all things that any normal entity couldn't do without a pile of permits, contracts, and affidavits as well as countless harassing visits from the Department of Transportation, the Water and Sewer Authority, the Better Business Bureau, the Audubon Society, and the Bureau of Alcohol, Tobacco and Firearms.[26]

Disney World eventually established production facilities for its branch brands: the Disney Channel and Nickelodeon among them. Universal followed with its own production complex. Disney–MGM Studios (since renamed Disney Hollywood Studios) has two components: Walt Disney Feature Animation Florida, where *Mulan* and *Lilo & Stitch* were produced, and Walt Disney Studios Florida, its soundstages used for films (*Passen-*

ger 57 starring Wesley Snipes), and TV productions including the Mickey Mouse Club, pro wrestling and special editions of game shows like *Wheel of Fortune*.

But more impressive is that Disney World blew the doors wide open for other entertainment ventures. Today, Orlando is one great big distraction after the other. That green tract Disney saw from the air in 1963 is now an unnatural wonder, an Andes of fiberglass, neon, and frosted glass. There are now attractions that relate to anyone and everyone: water and marine enthusiasts (Wet 'n Wild, Sea World), astrophiles (Kennedy Space Center), sports lovers (ESPN Zone, NASCAR Café), and Bible thumpers (the Holy Land Experience, complete with a scaled-down version of Jesus-era Jerusalem and virtual reality simulation of the Rapture). More than 50 million tourists come to Orlando every year, staying at the city's 500 hotels and eating at the 5,100 restaurants.[27]

Locations, Locations, Locations

Some towns didn't invite film as a permanent resident. They were more like tour stops for the traveling circus. Nowhere was that more true—literally—than in Sarasota. Now a posh Gulf-front hamlet that stretches from mainland to barrier island, years ago it was known solely as the winter home of the Ringling Brothers Barnum and Bailey Circus. John, the most famous of the five Ringling brothers, and wife Mabel moved the family business from New York to Sarasota in 1926. He used a portion of the family wealth to built Ca d'Zan, his own Medici palace: thirty-two rooms filled with Ringling's growing collection of Renaissance, Rococo, and Baroque masterpieces.

Another great showman had his eye on Sarasota as well—Cecil B. DeMille. In 1950, one circus met another when DeMille took Paramount's money to Sarasota to make *The Greatest Show on Earth*, essentially a circus performer showcase with a script written around it. And it worked. Technicolor brought every last sequin and dyed feather to life. Although DeMille and his crew followed the circus on the road and to Cedar City, Utah, for the grand finale, much of the six-week shoot was spent in Florida.

The film made it obvious that DeMille revered the circus; he wasn't after the freak show. The opening montage is accompanied by a voiceover: "We bring you the circus, the pied piper whose magic tunes lead children of all

A crowd gathers outside a Sarasota theater for the premiere of Cecil B. DeMille's *The Greatest Show on Earth*. It was filmed at the Ringling property in Sarasota. *Florida Photographic Collection, Tallahassee, Florida*

ages, from six to sixty, into a tinsel and spun-candy world of reckless beauty, of mounting laughter, whirling thrills, of rhythm, excitement and grace, of daring and glaring and dance." Although the film stars Charlton Heston as the circus's manager and Jimmy Stewart as Buttons, the clown haunted by his past, the credits highlight more than sixty performers, among them Bones Brown, Miss Loni, Mroczkowski's Liberty Horses, Tiebur's Sea Lions, the Flying Artonis, the Flying Concellos, and the Flying Comets.

The Greatest Show on Earth premiered under the Big Top in Sarasota with half the town in attendance. At the 1952 Academy Awards, it won Best Picture. The film was DeMille's penultimate picture. His final shot would be with Heston in his biggest Oscar bonanza, *The Ten Commandments*.

Another place that made its name with one flick is Wakulla Springs, a tiny town south of Tallahassee located where the panhandle meets the pan. The city's natural springs, which gave the town its name, doubled as the Ama-

Ricou Browning puts on his costume as he prepares to shoot *Creature from the Black Lagoon* in Wakulla Springs. *Florida Photographic Collection, Tallahassee, Florida*

The poster for *Creature from the Black Lagoon*, the 1954 camp horror classic shot in Wakulla Springs. *Collection of the Museum of Florida History, Florida Department of State*

zon River and the Gill-Man's hideout in *Creature from the Black Lagoon*, the 1954 camp horror classic. Ben Chapman donned the emerald rubber when the Gill-Man was out of the water, and Fort Pierce native Ricou Browning, Olympic swimmer and producer of the mermaid shows in Weeki Wachee Spring, played the Gill-Man in the water. Neither were credited. The movie was such a hit that it spawned two sequels, *Revenge of the Creature* and *The Creature Walks Among Us*. Fifty years later, Wakulla Springs is still celebrating. Every year it holds CreatureFest, a film festival dedicated to one of the most famous movie monsters of all time. The two-day event concludes with a drive-in–style screening of the original film in Wakulla Springs State Park. And don't forget to visit the snack bar: "Our fish have been caught by the Gill Man himself!"[28]

᪥ ᪦

By 1930, Jacksonville had lost its major film players: William Fox, William Selig, Gene Gauntier, Oliver Hardy, and others. It had even lost film stars it didn't know it had, including Merian Cooper, born in Jacksonville in 1893. A Navy pilot turned war hero turned producer, Cooper's film career started overseas, making documentary films with partner Ernest Schoedsack. Their film adventures included an elephant stampede in Persia and the capture of a man-eating tiger in Siam. Cooper channeled his love for exotic adrenalin into *King Kong*, the 1933 fantasy-horror classic he co-directed with Schoedsack.[29] But he didn't film it in Jacksonville.

The state got a glimmer of hope in 1934, and it came from California. Although he was plenty famous from writing his 1906 book *The Jungle*, Upton Sinclair had not been successful in his attempts to occupy a public office. He unsuccessfully ran for the U.S. House of Representatives in 1920 and the U.S. Senate in 1922. In the spring of 1934, he joined the California gubernatorial race. He defeated eight contenders en route to winning the Democratic Party nomination. Many film industry heavyweights hated the idea of Sinclair winning; although he campaigned as a Democrat, they all knew he was a Socialist at heart. People like Douglas Fairbanks and Joe Schenck (film executive and co-founder of the Academy of Motion Picture Arts and Sciences) worried about LA being victim to a Communist takeover. Schenck and Fairbanks promised to move the industry to Florida if Sinclair won. A recruiting visit to Miami underscored their seriousness.

When Louis B. Mayer was asked about the possibility of moving, he said, "That is something to be considered if and when the time comes." Republican Frank Merriam defeated Sinclair handily, and the threat never materialized.[30]

Meanwhile, Jacksonville was building film cachet in other ways, the greatest of which was the construction of the Florida Theatre. When it opened to the public on April 8, 1927, the Florida Theatre was Jacksonville's fifteenth movie theater. It was also the largest and most aesthetically grandiose in the state. It's like an opera house built into the set of *Romeo and Juliet*: grand balconies, soft amber lighting, planters embedded in the walls, all executed with a blend of Mediterranean and Moorish flavor. When the *Florida Times-Union* announced the Florida Theatre's arrival and its prominent placement on the corner of Forsyth and Newnan Streets, it stated it was "one of the South's finest playhouses," adding, "in addition to the theater itself there is an attractive roof garden commanding a beautiful view of the city and the St. Johns River."[31] Over the past eighty years, more than 4,000 movies and events have graced the space, drawing some 3.8 million people. Thanks to several artists who appeared there, the theater is now a landmark. It was here in 1956 that Elvis Presley held his first indoor concert. The event and the theater were featured in *Life Magazine*, largely because Jacksonville Juvenile Court judge Marion Gooding watched the performance to make sure the King's body movements weren't too suggestive.[32]

By the 1930s, Richard Norman was still working, still in film, but had downsized tremendously. Save for the few industrial films he produced, Norman was solely focused on distribution, oftentimes to schools that converted their gymnasiums into movie theaters at night. Norman was still in the business of serving black institutions and organizations. In 1939, he responded to a movie request from the South Miami Colored School. "We have an excellent Talking Picture Program in Joe Louis, featured in *Roar Of The Crowd*, shown with a talking western and comedy," wrote Norman.[33] In the opening frames of *Roar of the Crowd*, the documentary of Joe Louis's many fights, the pugilist is introduced: "The Brown Bomber, the Tan Menace, the Tawny Tornado." In the match against Max Baer, the Jewish fighter with a satin Star of David on his trunks, the ring announcer states, "May I respectfully think that . . . the sincere feeling in your heart be that regardless of race, creed or color, let us all say and mean it, may the better man emerge victorious." Louis beat Baer, but a poor showing against German Max Schmeling in 1936 followed. "Even the best of them have their off night," reads the title card. A year later, Joe Louis won back his championship title, something Jacksonville never did.

Richard Edward Norman passed away in 1961. Fifteen years later, Gloria Norman sold Norman Studios.

⇥ 10 ⇤

Jacksonville: Act Three

Why'd any monster want to come to this town anyway?
—Teenage boyfriend, *Zaat*, 1971

A weightless safe for bank robbery scenes. A propeller from a World War I fighter plane. Clocks and tea sets. Civil War hats and hospital gurneys.

It was November 4, 1976, and Norman Studios was being liquidated. Gloria Norman was finally selling the acre-and-a-half property—five buildings and a buried swimming pool priced at $165,000. Someone would certainly snatch up the property in the emerging neighborhood, especially now that Arlington connected to downtown Jacksonville via the Mathews Bridge. But what about all the movie props and mementos? They were being auctioned off at B&R Auctions on Edgewood Avenue. Some things went quick, like the taxidermied armadillo and the toy movie camera Norman had built for his young son. Other items, not so much: the 1930s mobile home and 54-horsepower gas motor were among the last items to go. Gloria Norman was on hand for it all, watching people bid on her husband's things, a memory walking out the door every few minutes.[1]

Nancy McAlister, a writer for the *Jacksonville Journal*, chatted with Mrs. Norman while it was all happening. She was funny and tender and nostalgic.

She recalled "having to keep the noise level down during [dance] lessons as so not to disturb the moviemaking. 'That was when they first started making talkies,' she said smiling."[2]

This was how Jacksonville's filmmaking history was going to end, with people picking through the scraps. These items individually meant nothing, but add them together—tea cups in the movie set's kitchen, a 54-horsepower motor to run the lights, a Civil War hat for the actor entering stage right—and it's the story of a film studio that made movies and history. But at least McAlister's article brought the city's story of filmmaking to the surface. It had been years, decades, since Jacksonville had been a movie town. By 1976, the memories were of memories.

Over the past half-century, Jacksonville has tried to revamp that long-gone film magic. Film projects have been and are still being made here—always sporadically, sometimes randomly—but there hasn't been consistency or quality. Just like it was in 1908, it's a town of epic sunlight and various looks that attract filmmakers. But Los Angeles is where the infrastructure is. How can David compete with Goliath when he hasn't slung a rock in five decades?

Jacksonville's film history from 1955 to 2007 is a story of location, whim, politics, courting, bidding, and circumstance. But the "World's Winter Film Capital" no longer exists. There's a difference between a film town and a town where films are made. Jacksonville is the latter, fighting places with similar DNA—New Orleans, Atlanta, the Carolinas—for a chance at the economic windfall that movies bring to a community. But the city can't build Rome now, even though we have more than a day to do so.

Historian Gary R. Mormino frankly discusses just how troubled Jacksonville was at mid-century:

> Throughout the 1950s and 1960s . . . perhaps no other city in Florida confronted more troubling crises than Jacksonville. Urban sprawl was feeding the suburbs and cutting off downtown. Between 1950 and 1965, the city's population actually fell from 204,500 to 196,000, while Duval County added 150,000 new residents. . . . Interstate 95 facilitated the movement of workers, shoppers, and new residents, but left behind in the lengthening shadows of its overpasses were deteriorating black

neighborhoods like LaVilla and Brooklyn. Jacksonville's reputation as a military town with a gritty edge turned away tourists and retirees. A bitter racial divide and a failing educational system threatened Jacksonville and Duval County.[3]

While Los Angeles was no saint—racial issues slowly simmered in South Central until finally erupting during the Watts riots in 1965 and again after the Rodney King verdict in 1992—its exponentially growing economy was a distraction from its shortcomings. By 1950, studio contracts were out and the star system was in. The public now clamored to the box office to see the faces, not just stories and show tunes. What business was booming in Jacksonville in 1950? Insurance. With the arrival of Prudential, State Farm, and others, the city earned the nickname of "the Insurance Center of the Southeast." There isn't an industry with less sex appeal. Have you ever seen a tourist ask a claims adjuster for an autograph?

As Hollywood boomed, Jacksonville became a caricature of its former self, a star who took any role that came down the pike. B-level horror became a common genre in Jacksonville starting in 1955. When *Creature from the Black Lagoon* was a cult hit, the sequel soon followed. For *Revenge of the Creature*, the crew moved west from Wakulla Springs to Jacksonville. In this 3-D black-and-white camp extravaganza, the Gill-Man (Ricou Browning returns behind the rubber mask) is captured by scientists and taken to an aquarium where he is abused and tortured (look for Clint Eastwood, uncredited as one of the aquarium lab rats). As the *Florida Times-Union* review put it, "these guys chug down to Gill Man's lagoon, where he ain't botherin' a soul, and dynamite the lagoon, killing a million fish and knocking the Gill Man into a coma that lasts until they get him transported to Marineland."[4]

The climax takes place at the Lobster House; the *Florida Times-Union* described it as a happy-hour shanty with "knotty pine paneling and . . . fishnet decor." Located on the south side of the St. Johns, halfway between the Main Street and Acosta bridges, it was a place "to drop by after work, meet a pal or a beau, have a drink and watch the sun go down and the skyline across the river fade out and then turn on with neon light." Today, the Lobster House is gone.[5]

Watch the film, and you'll see "Gill Man break up a party at the Lobster House. He bursts in, grabs Lori Nelson, whom he loves, dives into the water and heads upstream with the blonde in tow." The Lobster House scene is full of extras with beehive hairdos and cat's-eye glasses.[6]

Sixteen years later, with Jacksonville cast as a nuclear swamp, more creatures crawled from its shores onto the big screen. But the 1971 film *Zaat* didn't have quite the following that *Creature* did. Produced by Barton Film Company, *Zaat* follows the trope of the megalomaniacal scientist that Mary Shelley created in 1817. "A mad scientist, craving respect and revenge, turns himself into a huge radioactive catfish—and proceeds to terrorize picturesque North Florida." The creature, somehow, is less attractive than the Gill-Man. With his extraterrestrial almond-shaped eyes and cauliflower pate, it's an Elephant Man who can hold his breath for a really, really long time (just like the *Creature* sequel, *Zaat* shot all its underwater scenes at Marineland in St. Augustine). If you can find a copy, keep an eye out for the teenage boyfriend who doesn't believe in uranium-marinated sea life. He utters a line that inadvertently rails against everything J.E.T. Bowden, Gene Gauntier, and Henry Klutho had built. After kissing his girlfriend, he asks her, "I don't believe in any of that stuff. Why'd any monster want to come to this town anyway?"[7]

When Jacksonville had the chance to take on major talent, it let it slip through its fingers. In 1965, Universal Marion, a fledgling production company that had made its money building heavy equipment, had a meeting scheduled with a young comic named Mel Brooks. Steve Wilson, a Universal Marion executive, and his partner Sidney Glazier (who'd just won an Academy Award for his documentary *The Eleanor Roosevelt Story*) met with Brooks at the Beauclerc Country Club. The reason for the meeting was a script Brooks had written called *Springtime for Hitler*. Wilson loved it and wanted to produce it. Brooks acted out the entire script at the table, every voice and character, which cemented the deal. Renamed *The Producers* to placate some nervous execs, the film was a modest success, suffering mostly for having been released the same year as the zeitgeist-shaping hit *The Graduate*. Universal Marion only produced one more Brooks project, the 1970 film *The 12 Chairs*. The company, a bunch of construction equipment executives who were ignorant about movies, eventually sold off its film division. "Four years later, in 1974, Mel Brooks made his third film, a gigantic hit called *Blazing Saddles*. It played about six months straight in Jacksonville. . . . Universal Marion funded another comedian's first directing effort—*Take The Money And Run*, by a stand-up comic named Woody Allen."[8] But even if Jacksonville had held onto Brooks and Allen for dear life, the two would have fought to escape: the proper support and infrastructure for their careers was out west, not here.

Florida as a whole didn't fare much better in the 60s and 70s. It was mostly home to blink-and-you-missed-them TV series. *Miami Undercover* and the ABC series *Surfside 6* (three detectives living on a houseboat) were shot in South Florida. *Tallahassee 7000* starred Walter Matthau as a Florida sheriff's investigator. *I Dream of Jeanie* was set in Cocoa Beach (Larry Hagman's character, astronaut Tony Nelson, was commuting to nearby Kennedy Space Center). But the show only used the beach town for establishing shots. After playing the Gill-Man in the *Creature* series, Ricou Browning joined forces with Miami producer Ivan Tors. Browning served as director, writer, stunt man, and stunt coordinator at Tors Studios, working on projects like *Sea Hunt*, *The Aquanauts*, and the *Flipper* movies and TV series.

By the 1980s, Florida was taking action to bring movie crews to the city. According to the Florida Motion Picture and Television Bureau, the state spent $430,000 annually (on promotion, advertising, travel to the West Coast, etc.) during the 80s to lure movie studios away from LA. Ben Harris, representative for the Florida Motion Picture and Television Bureau, told the *Florida Times-Union* in 1984, "Movie companies can save 25 percent overall by filming in the Sunshine State." Harris was quick to add that shooting in Los Angeles came with a web of red tape. "The Los Angeles area contains 83 municipalities, each with its own fees and regulations. . . . Greed has become a factor. A homeowner in California may charge a movie company $5,000 just to use the inside of a home."[9] For its efforts Jacksonville was rewarded with a few films, but the city never caught any real traction. In 1986, Steve Guttenberg and Bubba Smith hit their marks in Alltel Stadium for *Police Academy IV: Citizens on Patrol*. Rob Lowe was in town the same year for the Peter Bogdanovich–directed *Illegally Yours*, where Lowe plays Richard Dice, a juror who falls in love with a woman on trial for murder.

From 1990 through 2005, business improved, thanks in part to the Jacksonville Film and Television Office, which, according to its Web site, "works with local film, digital media and related businesses to enhance job creation and economic development throughout the region." It considers motion pictures, television movies, commercials, and music videos to be an "essential part" of its focus.[10]

"A world of locations in one city," reads the first page of the Jacksonville Film and Television Office's brochure. For the 2004 remake of *The Manchurian Candidate*, starring Denzel Washington, St. George Episcopal Church on historic Fort George Island doubled for Louisiana. For Joel Schumacher's *Tigerland*, about army recruits training for the Vietnam War, Camp Blanding stood in for Fort Polk in Louisiana. Schumacher, who directed *St. Elmo's Fire*, *The Lost Boys*, and *A Time to Kill*, held a press conference at Camp Blanding in 2000, where he shared his thoughts about the city's benefits and limits. "I don't think you could do Paris in the 1940s, or climbing Mount Everest," Schumacher said. "But I think that if more people in my industry knew what was available here, they'd come here in droves."[11] Three years earlier, Camp Blanding had been the location for the Demi Moore vehicle *G.I. Jane*.

But let's be honest: an army base is an army base. What's most surprising is how Jacksonville has doubled for places that the naked eye couldn't find in the city. For *The Devil's Advocate*, the 1997 thriller where Keanu Reeves plays a hotshot Southern lawyer and Al Pacino plays Beelzebub in a Joseph Abboud suit, downtown Jacksonville doubles for New York City. That same year, actor Charles S. Dutton (*Rudy*, *Menace II Society*) made his directorial debut with *First Time Felon*. For this HBO miniseries, Jacksonville is Chicago, with the St. Johns as the Chicago River's stunt double.

For *The New Adventures of Pippi Longstocking*, the sandy bluffs and historic architecture of nearby Amelia Island served as New England. In 1997, the city became Panama: the jungle thickets of Cecil Commerce Park stood in for the Central American rain forest in *Basic*, the John Travolta–Samuel L. Jackson thriller directed by John McTiernan. But sometimes it's okay to be yourself. The city's most recent TV project was the History Channel miniseries *Conquest of America*, produced in 2004. The episode "Conquest of the Southeast" relived the Spanish slaying of the French Huguenots at Matanzas Inlet in 1565. If you were on set at Guana River State Park, you'd have seen actors in metal armor marching over the bodies of other actors in linen tunics.

According to the Jacksonville Film and Television Office, film production generated $99 million in revenue in 2003. Its Web site breaks down the regional impact of a feature film (based on a fourteen-week shooting schedule) by line items specifying how much each cog of a production can bring in.

Housing (including hotels, apartments, and homes)	$480,902
Technicians and local crew (labor)	$13,000,000
Actors (extras, local hires)	$53,179
Catering (food distribution companies)	$50,033
Set construction costs	$239,441
Studio/stage rental	$33,148
Special heavy equipment rentals	$161,168
Film processing	$7,000
Location fees	$9,600
Miscellaneous (gas, utilities, cleaning, waste mgmt.)	$9,600
GRAND TOTAL	$14,044,071[12]

But there is something less tangible than money that makes local film-making important. That is the place as icon. While one film shoot can pour millions of dollars into a local community, the right film can make a city. "*Miami Vice* had every bit to do with the resurrection of South Beach," says Todd Roobin, head of the Jacksonville Film and Television Office. "I hear about other great success stories. *Field of Dreams* and that Iowa cornfield, the bench that Forrest Gump sat on in Savannah. People want to go and see those locations."[13] That's tourism and hospitality, heads in beds and restaurants. That's the economics every town looks for. Unfortunately, Jacksonville hasn't been made by the movies.

⤳ ⤶

Ann Burt's morning routine began with a walk. She would leave her home in sneakers and take to the roads of historic Arlington, all quiet save for the faintest din of traffic on the Mathews Bridge. She passed four old buildings on Arlington Road every day for a long time. Finally, a friend told her they were part of an old studio that had made silent movies. The fifth structure, the indoor set building on the back side of the lot, now belonged to Circle of Faith Ministries and its predominantly African American congregation. As she learned more about the Norman story from her neighbors, she became more passionate about the survival of the buildings. The Norman story had the potential to save Arlington and make it something more than just a final resting place for strip malls, auto detailers, and beauty salons.

"Historic preservation and economic revitalization go hand in hand," says Burt, former president of Old Arlington, Inc., the nonprofit aimed at protecting and promoting the suburb through history, education, and economic development. "We all knew the Norman studios were important, that it was nationally significant. The truth is the City of Jacksonville didn't know it."[14]

In 2001, the City of Jacksonville Planning and Development Department and JaxPride, a nonprofit organization dedicated to the beautification of Jacksonville's communities, put Arlington in its crosshairs. It was a suburb in need of help. According to the *Arlington Community Improvement Strategy for Old Town*, the community "displays the typical signs of aging postwar suburbs. This includes, generally, affordable housing, mature vegetation, strip development along the major roadways, and some deteriorating commercial and residential structures." In the section titled "The Vision," one item under the header "Economic Development" read simply: "Restore Norman Studios and develop a suitable use for the property."[15]

What the city didn't know what just how big a piece of history it was sitting on. Arlington claimed the nation's only silent film studio that was still on its feet. Barely. The owners that followed the Normans cared little for the property. If Hurricane David had come ashore in 1979, JaxPride's strategic plan would have been a eulogy.

Burt and Old Arlington, Inc. began working tirelessly to save the studio: filing for city and state grants (which came through) and gaining support from the local African American Chamber of Commerce (which never materialized). The critical moment came when Burt convinced the National Trust for Historic Preservation to stop by Arlington on its way to vetting a property in Amelia Island. Burt recalls the presentation Old Arlington, Inc. made to the Trust. It was a disaster. There weren't enough printouts of the proposal. The PowerPoint presentation didn't work. "I was crushed beyond belief," Burt says.[16]

Even though Burt had written off any chance of an endorsement by the National Trust, they waited anxiously for the report. When it arrived, according to Burt, it stated that Norman Studios "is of national significance and should be viewed by the community as such."[17]

"Saving Norman Studios is all about capturing your history because that's what gives you your sense of place, it's what makes us unique, and not just Arlington, but Jacksonville and Florida," says Burt. "Gene Gauntier talked about it in her memoirs. She called Kalem's trip to Jacksonville 'epoch-making.' That trip established the custom of [filmmakers] traveling far and wide in search of authentic locale."[18]

Old Arlington, Inc. had the blessing of the National Trust for Historic Preservation. The Jacksonville City Council had unanimously approved the purchase of Norman Studios. All they needed now was, well, Norman Studios. In 2002, it was still privately owned. In fact, the owner had gotten so tired of city involvement in his four buildings, which included sticking a "condemned" sign out front, that he threatened to tear it all down. "I drove by one day and saw the trucks with the wrecking company sign on the side," says Burt, who eventually calmed the owner down and convinced him to try just one more negotiation.[19]

In 2002, just before Christmas, the city of Jacksonville purchased Norman Studios. The price tag was $260,000. The property is currently under the jurisdiction of the Jacksonville Department of Parks, Recreation, Entertainment and Conservation (DPREC). The group has been in negotiations with Circle of Faith Ministries about acquiring the fifth building. According to DPREC representative Dan Kronrath, the church has identified a property it would like to move to. And the church is ready to move. Displayed during Sunday services is a watercolor rendering of a new sanctuary and multipurpose center.

Meanwhile, Norman's "national significance" was ballooning without the help of Arlington's community activists, the Jacksonville City Council, or the Department of Parks and Recreation. Six hundred forty-seven miles away from those five buildings, Richard Norman was on the wall at the Smithsonian.

⛤

Organized by the Smithsonian Institution and the Academy of Motion Picture Arts and Sciences, *Close Up in Black: African American Film Posters* featured ninety vintage and contemporary movie posters from the Edward Mapp Collection held by the Black Film Center/Archive at Indiana University, the same institution that owns many of Norman's original films, press sheets, and placards. The exhibit included "blaxploitation" classics like *Blacula*, *Foxy Brown*, and *Superfly*. There was an interesting pairing of two seemingly unconnected movies. On the gallery wall was the poster for *House-Rent Party* starring black performers Pigmeat Markam and John "Rastus" Murray. The 1946 comedy was ignored by white audiences and blackballed from white consciousness. Next to it was the 1990 film *House Party*, starring hip-hop duo Kid and Play. Aimed at black youth, *House Party* became a surprise crossover hit, spawning three sequels. Richard Norman claims three posters in the exhibit: *The Flying Ace*, *Black Gold*, and the deserted island thriller *Regeneration*.

The traveling exhibition was on the road for three years, from January 2003 to July 2005. It covered every corner of the map: Wolfsonian Museum in Miami Beach, the California African American Museum in Los Angeles, the American Jazz Museum in Kansas City, the National Heritage Museum in Lexington, Massachusetts, and the Mobile Museum of Art in Alabama. The finale was a three-month run at the Smithsonian in Washington, D.C.

The success of the exhibit was twofold: it made film posters credible as art, and it underscored the historic and modern influence of black cinema. Norman was critical to both: his posters were gorgeous watercolors with all kinds of action verbs clinched with exclamation points. His place in the *Close Up in Black* exhibit was unique because his were the pictures you expected from black filmmakers.

Jacksonville responded to the national recognition of Norman at the Smithsonian with *Real to Reel: The Fabulous Years of Silent Filmmaking in Florida*, an exhibit that opened at the Cummer Museum of Art and Gardens on August 5, 2004. The five-week exhibit featured Norman's film posters as well as memorabilia from other locally produced films: photographic stills, film reels, books, handbills, and written memoirs.

The Cummer held an evening screening of *Creature from the Black Lagoon* in conjunction with the exhibit. More than 500 guests crammed into the showing. Like some sort of vigil, like the muttered chant of a medium, those images of Wakulla Springs summoned spirits from decades past. Suddenly, doors flew open and memories flooded the room. When the lights came up, the museum's curators were bombarded with snippets of stories. "We've had this old film canister in our attic for years, never knowing why we had it or where it came from." "My grandmother said she was in a movie when she was little, but we never believed her." Robert Broward, Jacksonville's foremost architectural historian, relayed his snippet to the Cummer's quarterly magazine: "During filming, anything could happen in Jacksonville. One time, my father witnessed a car filled with people driving off the end of a river ferry, never knowing it was a movie stunt."[20] These are all pieces to a puzzle the city still hasn't solved.

֎

It's the day you've been waiting for and you're an hour early. A slow drive through town will kill the time.

Arlington looks like it fell into a Sleeping Beauty nap circa 1960 and still hasn't been kissed by the prince. Everywhere you look the metal is rusted, the paint is chipped and peeling, and signs use fonts once used to sell soda fountains and whitewall tires. Bomb shelter is the pervading architectural style. The Excelling Stars of Tomorrow Learning Center, a low-rise blue cinderblock box, neighbors a hair salon, a low-rise pink cinderblock box.

Arlington also boasts a cluster of churches. Arlington Baptist, with a steeple so white it makes the clouds look dirty, neighbors the Church of Christ, Arlington Presbyterian, and Iglesia ni Cristo.

Norman Studios is across the street from a homeless shelter. When the property became a home to squatters who don't take residence at the shelter, the city installed a security system and wrapped the acre in chain-link fence. As you get out for a closer look, a woman in the distance screams like a tea kettle.

Looking from the street, one of the first things you notice are the old live oaks dangling clumps of Spanish moss as long as a bride's train. The buildings are much less extroverted. Save for Gloria Norman's colorful Dance School sign, which faces passing traffic, there's no hint that this place was what it was. Ann Burt doesn't blame people for having no idea they're driving by history. "It's hard for people to get the national significance of this, because they just don't see it, figuratively and literally," she says. "There's not even a sign on the door to know there's something there."[21]

When Dan Kronrath, a representative of the Jacksonville Parks and Recreation Department, pulls up, he shares a handshake and a flashlight. After unlocking the deadbolt, he pushes the wobbly gate through a layer of leaves and detritus.

The buildings are set up like houses and hotels on a Monopoly board: the four structures face each other, a square, backyard-sized plot of grass in the center (dig and you'll find the buried swimming pool). Unlike those on Boardwalk and Park Place, these buildings are in awful disrepair. The actors' changing cottage, about the size of a mobile home, leans in against itself for support; its knees could buckle under a stiff wind. The studio production building facing Arlington Road is one layer of plywood skin over another. The first-floor windows have been boarded up.

Inside, the walls are rotting from water damage. Insulation hangs from the ceiling. The wood floors are torn up, planks scattered and splintered. The screening room is recognizable only because of the hole in the wall (for the projector's lens) and the white box on the other side of the room (where the dailies were screened).

The prop garage in the back of the lot holds the most clues to the past. When you enter the first thing you see is a huge, combine-sized engine for powering Klieg lights. The flashlight illuminates a sign on the wall: "Theater Equipped. Lease or for Sale. Contact Your Broker or R. E. Norman, Jr." And there, on the floor, is a pile of rusted film reels and canisters. Using your fingers, you feel "Kodak" on one of the lids.

From the front door of the prop garage, the indoor set building can be seen clearly. Today, it's Circle of Faith Ministries, beautifully restored and polar-white. It has the same dollhouse windows it always did, but some modern alterations have been made (ramp for the handicapped, new windows, dense metal doors). Inside, chandeliers with Sputnik-like prongs hang from the ceiling. Fake plants flank the pulpit. It shows no signs of belonging to film history. Maybe if the city buys it back, the makeup will be wiped off. If people are lucky, they'll recognize the face underneath.

The sad look of Norman Studios betrays the work that's been done to it. According to the DPREC, much of the grant money has been spent: $20,000 for emergency roofing, $2,155 for security lighting, and $2,855.94 for the security system.

The largest chunk—$50,201.43—was paid to Kenneth Smith Architects, the Jacksonville architecture firm charged with redesigning the property for its future life as the Norman Studios Silent Film Museum. The watercolor rendering, perhaps coincidentally, looks like it was pulled from Norman's letterhead of seventy years ago.

Devan Stuart is the chair of the Norman Studios Silent Film Museum. She is the head of the board: fifteen people, all of whom are white. One of them is Norman's son, Richard Jr., a retired airline pilot. "I'm a white girl," says Stuart with a laugh. "We need a racial mix on the board. The most wonderful thing about this property's history is that it allowed blacks to participate in the industry. We need our board to reflect that."[22]

The restoration of the Norman property, slated for completion in 2008, will feature a number of elements. Part of it will be a silent film museum, exhibiting the organization's current holdings (such as framed Norman movie

NORMAN STUDIOS RESTORATIONS
FOR THE CITY OF JACKSONVILLE

KENNETH SMITH ARCHITECTS, INC.

A watercolor rendering of the Norman Studios Silent Film Museum. *Courtesy Kenneth Smith Architects, Jacksonville*

posters, old film equipment, promotional materials, props, and a Keystone Kops helmet). There will also be a live production facility where local film-makers can screen their movies and the museum can host acting and directing workshops. "We'd also like to have a summer camp for at-risk kids. They'd come here on scholarship and we'd teach them about the film industry. The kids would also be responsible for making a film, with each of them handling a different responsibility. The final product would be for the kids, but it's something to show at fund-raising galas as well."[23]

But like all things in show business, Stuart knows this project could be made easier with a celebrity attached. So far, no one has shown interest. "We approached Bill Cosby a few years back," says Stuart. "I know he's familiar with Norman's story. He was recently in a bidding war with the Museum of Science and History over a camera or similar artifact. His people told us he wasn't interested, but they wished us well."[24] Similar results came from Will Smith's camp. Stuart is hoping to cultivate a connection to Samuel L. Jackson.

John Culbreath, head of the Department of Parks and Recreation, attended Morehouse College with the *Pulp Fiction* star.

With or without a celebrity endorsement, the Norman Studios Museum is moving at a snail's pace. In Old Arlington, Inc.'s January 2007 newsletter, there was a tiny paragraph dedicated to the project's status. "Ann Burt, representing OAI on the steering committee, expressed the frustration of the community over the long unexplained delay of this project."[25]

Columbia Studios, on Washington Boulevard in Culver City, California, is an Olympic homage. Its main gate is an assemblage of hanging chandeliers, Doric columns, Roman arches, and security guards behind mirrored lenses. Sharp fencing made of metal stakes wards off trespassers. Those on foot have to walk for thirty minutes—a sitcom's length—to get around it. Neighboring Sony Pictures offers much of the same in both size and breadth but adds a smoked glass ziggurat dubbed Sony Pictures Plaza.

Universal City is so large that its name is its address: Universal City, California. A royal blue sign greets you: "Welcome to Universal Studios Hollywood—The Entertainment Capital of L.A." On the lot, there are the actual sets for *Jurassic Park* and *The Mummy* but also "Jurassic Park: The Ride" and "The Revenge of the Mummy: The Ride." There are bars, clubs, restaurants, movie theaters, amphitheaters, and hotels.

Warner Brothers Studios in Burbank, featuring 100 acres of sound stages and 20 acres of outdoor sets, isn't much smaller than the mountains behind it. This fact is underscored by the studio façade's cartoon mural: Bugs Bunny, Fred Flintstone, Superman, and Wile E. Coyote replace Washington, Jefferson, Roosevelt and Lincoln as the faces on Mount Rushmore.

To see these monolithic dream factories and then to see Norman Studios looking like a child's popsicle-stick dollhouse is to easily measure where each city went after the competition was over. Los Angeles owns every media we see. Take for instance Warner Brothers: it's not just the movies (which includes Warner Brothers, Morgan Creek, and Castle Rock), it's television (the CW), music (Atlantic, Maverick, and Reprise Records), and archives (Hanna Barbara and Marvel Comics). The rabbit hole only gets deeper. Time Warner, the conglomerate that owns Warner Brothers, has under its media umbrella AOL, MapQuest, CNN, HBO, Cinemax, TNT, New Line Cinema, Cartoon Network, Comedy Central, *Time, Southern Living, Fortune,* and *Sports Illustrated.* Total number of employees: 96,000.[26]

You won't find any such thing in Jacksonville or in Florida, for that matter. Save for the one-off motion picture (*Miami Vice*) or television show (*Miami Vice*), there is no media power here. The state is working hard to change that. Shortly after taking office in 2007, Governor Charlie Crist recommended investing $75 million for each of the next three years to promote film and entertainment productions in Florida, an annual budgetary increase of $55 million. The $20 million allocated for fiscal year 2006–2007 attracted thirty-two productions and generated more than $133 million in revenue for the local economy, representing a return on investment of $6.60 for every dollar spent.[27]

That push is desperately needed. In January 2007, the Governor's Office of Film and Entertainment reported that *Addictive Fishing* was filming in Melbourne. Brenton Productions of Tampa was shooting *Truck Universe* and *Hi-Rev Tuners,* a television show about building souped-up compact cars. Also on the list were high-profile TV series such as *CSI: Miami* and Show-time's *Dexter,* about a serial-killing blood-splatter expert for the Miami Police Department. Except for those two shows, the state is used mostly for B-roll exteriors. Adding insult to injury, somewhere on an LA studio back lot there's a soundstage filled with sand, coconut palms, and Art Deco neon.

The movies built Los Angeles. They are responsible for the manses of Beverly Hills, the view from Mulholland Drive, and attractions such as the Walk of Fame and Grauman's Chinese Theater. The Los Angeles Convention and Visitors Bureau reported that in 2005 it hosted 25 million visitors, generating a total of $12.9 billion in spending. The Jacksonville Convention and Visitors Bureau makes no mention of its annual statistics. Searching for Norman Studios on its Web site is a futile endeavor. It's not under "Attractions" or "Historic Landmarks." Maybe we can take solace in the fact that Los Angeles is only the fourth largest destination for domestic travel in the United States. Orlando is number two.[28]

While it may not resemble a glittering pool—from atop Griffith Park, Los Angeles at night looks like the perfect place to pan for gold—Jacksonville is a growing metropolis. According to the Jacksonville Economic Development Commission, the downtown area has eighteen residential properties under way, providing all manner of living: condominiums, lofts, town homes, penthouses, and so forth.[29] The St. John, the proposed 50-story residential high-rise in chic Southbank, the city's emerging SoHo, will be the tallest structure in the city (besting the 42-story Bank of America building). The St. Johns River, still the city's star, has several major corporate headquarters along its banks, including the Haskell Company, the nation's largest design-build company, and the St. Joe Company, Florida's largest private landowner (the real estate conglomerate owns 800,000 acres in North Florida—that's 200 times the size of Miami Beach). But the city still has some growing to do. When Super Bowl XXXIX came to town in 2005, there weren't enough hotel rooms in close proximity to Alltel Stadium. To accommodate all the guests, the city chartered five cruise ships to serve as floating hotels.

The drive from the St. Johns waterfront to Circle of Faith Ministries bisects Jacksonville's tiny downtown. The trapezoidal Modus building rises like a chimney; Jacksonville Landing, a largely ignored alfresco shopping pavilion, is the hearth at its feet. From this riverfront perspective, a glance across the St. Johns reveals one bridge after the other after the other, each casting the metallic din of steady traffic across the glassy black water. The FECR bridge, trademarked by crisscrossed steel supports, is the enduring legacy of Henry Flagler's expansion plan. The Main Street Bridge, also known as the John Alsop, glows blue at night. When you stand underneath it, the constant traffic makes it sound like the rattling of old bones.

Arlington is peeling, dusty, and rusting. So are the last pieces of the last silent film studio in America. That is, except for the one belonging to Circle of Faith Ministries. Here, members of Pastor Joseph McRoy's congregation pray and shout on the same floors where, a lifetime earlier, actors did the same thing. The only difference is one is made of faith and devotion, the other of emulsion and silver halide.

Appendix

Films Made in Jacksonville: 1908–1926

According to Law (Gaumont, 1916)
Adventures of the Girl Spy (Kalem, 1909)
The Adventures of Duffy (Eagle, 1916)
The Advocate (Gambier, 1915)
All in a Day (Vim, 1916)
Ambitious Awkward Andy (Thanhouser, 1916)
The Arab's Bride (Thanhouser, 1912)
Armadale (Gaumont, 1916)
The Artist and the Girl (Kalem, 1909)
Artists and Models (Lubin, 1915)
Backstage (King Bee, 1917)
Back to the Primitive (Selig, 1911)
The Baroness (Thanhouser, 1916)
A Battle of Bloody Ford (Kalem, 1912)
Battle of Pottsburg Bridge (Kalem, 1912)
Battle of Virginia Hills (Kalem, 1912)
The Battle of Wits (Kalem, 1912)
Between Love and Duty (Kalem, 1910)

The Booze Dream (Eagle, 1916)
The Breath of Scandal (Kalem, 1912)
Broadway Jones (Cohan, 1917)
Brother's Equal (Thanhouser, 1916)
The Buccaneers (Selig, 1911)
Busted Hearts (Vim, 1916)
Carriage of Death (Thanhouser, 1916)
Chains Invisible (Equitable, 1916)
Charlie's Aunt (Lubin, 1915)
Chickens (Vim, 1916)
A Circus Romance (Equitable, 1916)
The Clarion (Equitable, 1916)
Classmates (Biograph, 1914)
The Colonel's Escape (Kalem, 1912)
The Colonel's Son (Kalem, 1911)
The Confederate Ironclad (Kalem, 1912)
Confederate Spy (Kalem, 1910)
The Cracker's Bride (Kalem, 1909)
Daughter of Dixie (Kalem, 1910)
The Deacon's Daughter (Kalem, 1910)
A Desperate Chase (Kalem, 1912)
Donuts (King Bee, 1917)
The Drifter (Gaumont, 1916)
The Drug Terror (Lubin, 1916)
Drummergirl of Vicksburg (Kalem, 1912)
The Drunkard's Daughter (Kalem, 1909)
Duffy the Cop (Eagle, 1916)
The Egret Hunter (Kalem, 1910)
The Escape from Andersonville (Kalem, 1909)
The Evil Woman (Thanhouser, 1916)
The Farm Bully (Kalem, 1912)
The Fatal Legacy (Kalem, 1912)
Fighting Dan McCool (Kalem, 1912)
Fisherman's Granddaughter (Kalem, 1910)
Fishing in Florida (Lubin, 1912)
The Fish Pirates (Kalem, 1909)

Fixing a Flirt (Lubin, 1912)
A Florida Feud (Kalem, 1909)
A Florida Romance (Lubin, 1913)
The Flying Ace (Norman, 1926)
The Flying Switch (Kalem, 1912)
A Fool Was There (Fox, 1917)
For Love of an Enemy (Kalem, 1911)
The Fraud at the Hope Mine (Kalem, 1912)
Frenzied Finance (Vim, 1916)
Further Adventures of the Girl Spy (Kalem, 1910)
Game Warden's Test (Kalem, 1909)
The Girl and the Bandit (Kalem, 1910)
The Girl in the Caboose (Kalem, 1912)
The Girl Spy before Vicksburg (1910)
The Girl Thief (Kalem, 1910)
The Grim Tale of War (Kalem, 1912)
The Gulf Between (Technicolor, 1918)
Her Soldier Sweetheart (Kalem, 1910)
The Hero (Vim, 1916)
He Winked and Won (Vim, 1917)
The Hidden Valley (Thanhouser, 1916)
The High Cost of Turkey (Edison, 1914)
The High Diver (Kalem, 1909)
His Mother's Picture (Kalem, 1912)
A Hitherto Unrelated Incident of the Girl Spy (Kalem, 1911)
Honeymoon through Snow to Sunshine (Lubin, 1910)
I Accuse (Gaumont, 1916)
The Idol of the Stage (Gaumont, 1915)
Infamous Don Miguel (Kalem, 1912)
In Old Florida (Kalem, 1911)
In the Hands of the Law (Moss, 1917)
The Isle of Love (Gaumont, 1916)
Jenks and His Motorboat (Comet, 1912)
John Burns of Gettysburg (Kalem, 1912)
Kaplan Kidds Kiddies (Falstaff, 1916)
Let Sleeping Dogs Lie (Kalem, 1909)

The Little Circus Rider (Selig, 1911)

Little Soldier of '64 (Kalem, 1911)

Lost in the Jungle (Selig, 1911)

The Love Romance of the Girl Spy (Kalem, 1910)

Love Triumphs (Kalem, 1909)

Making of a Champion (Kalem, 1909)

Man and His Soul (Metro, 1916)

The Man Who Lost (Kalem, 1910)

Maternity (World-Brady, 1917)

Millionaire Tramp (Motograph, 1910)

The Miser's Child (Kalem, 1910)

A Mission of State (Kalem, 1916)

The Money Gulf (Kalem, 1915)

The Mother of Men (Olcott International, 1914)

Mother's Child (Lubin, 1915)

Mystery of Pine Tree Camp (Olcott-Gauntier, 1913)

My Wife's Birthday (Comet, 1912)

Nearly in Mourning (Lubin, 1912)

The New Minister (Kalem, 1909)

The Night Watch (Kalem, 1916)

The Northern Schoolmaster (Kalem, 1909)

The Nymph (Thanhouser, 1916)

The Ocean Pearl (Eagle, 1916)

The Octoroon (Kalem, 1909)

The Old Fiddler (Kalem, 1910)

The Old Soldier's Story (Kalem, 1909)

One Hour (Moss, 1917)

One on Romance (Lubin, 1912)

The Orange Grower's Daughter (Kalem, 1909)

The Ordeal of Elizabeth (Vitagraph, 1916)

The Other Sister (Equitable, 1916)

Outwitting Daddy (Lubin, 1913)

The Oval Diamond (Thanhouser, 1916)

The Paperhanger's Helper (Lubin, 1915)

Perils of Pauline (Astra, 1916)

Perkins Peace Party (Thanhouser, 1916)

A Pig in a Poke (Kalem, 1909)
Pipe Dream (Gaumont, 1916)
The Pirates of the Sky (Eagle, 1916)
Plump and Runt series (Vim, 1916)
The Pony Express Girl (Kalem, 1912)
A Poor Wife's Devotion (Kalem, 1909)
Prisoners of War (Kalem, 1912)
The Prison Shop (Kalem, 1912)
The Quality of Faith (Gaumont, 1915)
A Race with Time (Kalem, 1912)
The Railroad Conspiracy (Kalem, 1912)
The Railroad Inspector's Peril (Kalem, 1912)
The Railway Mail Clerk (Kalem, 1910)
Red Scorpion (Eagle, 1916)
Regeneration (Norman, 1923)
A Romance of the Everglades (Edison, 1914)
The Romance of the Trained Nurse (Kalem, 1910)
Rose of Old St. Augustine (Selig, 1911)
Saved from Court Martial (Kalem, 1913)
A Sawmill Hazard (Kalem, 1912)
The Scholar (Vim, 1916)
The Sea Dogs (Vim, 1916)
The Seminole Half-Breeds (Kalem, 1910)
The Seminole's Sacrifice (Selig, 1911)
Shadows of the Past (Selig, 1911)
She Must Be Ugly (Lubin, 1913)
Shipwrecked (Kalem, 1912)
The Slave Catchers of Florida (Kalem, 1909)
A Slave to Drink (Kalem, 1910)
The Smuggler's Daughter (Lubin, 1914)
Social Buccaneers (Kalem, 1916)
Social Highwaymen (Peerless, 1916)
South Sea Island (Mirror, 1916)
The Spark of Honor (Palm, 1916)
A Spartan Mother (Kalem, 1912)
Sporting Days in the South (Kalem, 1909)

The Spy (Selig, 1911)
The Stepmother (Kalem, 1910)
The Struggle (Equitable, 1916)
Sunshine and Tempest (Dixie, 1916)
The Survival of the Fittest (Selig, 1911)
Swami Sam (Lubin, 1915)
Taft for a Day (Motograph, 1910)
A Tale of a Rubber Boot (Comet, 1912)
Taming Wild Animals (Selig, 1910)
Theodore's Terrible Thirst (Thanhouser, 1916)
Thirty Days (Comet, 1912)
This Way Out (Vim, 1916)
The Tramps (Lubin, 1915)
A Treacherous Shot (Kalem, 1912)
The Tryout (Vim, 1916)
The Two Spies (Kalem, 1912)
Under a Flag of Truce (Kalem, 1912)
The Unfortunate Woman (Palm, 1916)
The Unpardonable Sin (World, 1916)
Ups and Downs (Vim, 1916)
Victim of Circumstance (Kalem, 1912)
The Water Cure (Vim, 1916)
The Water Devil (Thanhouser, 1916)
Water Soaked Hero (Lubin, 1913)
The Weight of a Crown (Lubin, 1916)
What Happened to Jones (World, 1915)
What's Sauce for the Goose (Vim, 1916)
When Men Hate (Olcott-Gauntier, 1913)
When the Men Left Town (Edison, 1914)
When Things Go Wrong (Kalem, 1916)
Wifie's Ma Comes Back (Lubin, 1915)
Witch of the Everglades (Selig, 1911)
The Woe of Battle (Kalem, 1912)
You Can't Beat Them (Lubin, 1914)

This abridged list does not include every film made in Jacksonville from 1908 through 1926. Many have been lost, destroyed, or damaged by time.

Sources

Klotman, Phyllis Rauch. *Frame By Frame—A Black Filmography*. Bloomington: Indiana University Press, 1979.

Nelson, Richard Alan. *Florida and the American Motion Picture Industry, 1898–1980*. 2 vols. New York: Garland Publishing, 1983.

Nelson, Richard Alan. *Lights! Camera! Florida! Ninety Years of Moviemaking and Television Production in the Sunshine State*. Tampa: Florida Endowment for the Humanities, 1987.

Reitzhammer, John B. "Jacksonville Titles." Compiled December 9, 1986. Film Collection at the Celeste Bartos Film Preservation Center, Museum of Modern Art Film Study Center, New York.

Ward, James Robertson. *Old Hickory's Town: An Illustrated History of Jacksonville*. Jacksonville: Florida Publishing Company, 1982.

Newspapers

Florida Times-Union
Jacksonville Journal

Notes

Chapter 1. New Year's Day, Twentieth Century

1. *Florida Times-Union*, January 1, 1900.
2. Ibid.
3. Crooks, *Jacksonville after the Fire*, 8–13.
4. Newton, *The Invisible Empire*, 3.
5. Davis, *History of Jacksonville, Florida, and Vicinity*, 486.
6. Wood, *Jacksonville's Architectural Heritage*, 50.
7. Foley and Wood, *The Great Fire of 1901*, 20.
8. Howe, *Winter Homes for Invalids*, 50–51.
9. Ward, *Old Hickory's Town*, 20.
10. Eliade, *Shamanism: Archaic Techniques of Ecstasy*, 271.
11. Davis, *History of Jacksonville, Florida, and Vicinity*, 1.
12. Hakluyt, *The Voyages, Traffiques, and Discoveries of Foreign Voyagers*, 89.
13. Davis, *History of Jacksonville, Florida, and Vicinity*, 111.
14. Ibid.
15. Ibid., 116.
16. Ibid., 118.
17. Rawls, "Ninety-Six Years of Engineering Development on the St. Johns River," 48–58.
18. Akin, *Flagler: Rockefeller Partner and Florida Baron*, 116–22.

19. Ibid., 134–42.

20. Davis, *History of Jacksonville, Florida, and Vicinity*, 491.

21. Crooks, 8.

22. *Florida Times-Union*, January 1, 1900.

23. Davis, *History of Jacksonville, Florida, and Vicinity*, 168.

24. Martin, *Consolidation: Jacksonville Duval County*, 176–78.

25. Ramsaye, *A Million and One Nights*, 59.

26. Ibid., 76.

27. Ezra, *Georges Méliès*, 1.

28. Ibid., 1–2.

29. Rittaud-Hutinet, *Letters: Auguste and Louis Lumière*, 31.

30. Ramsaye, *A Million and One Nights*, 281–87.

Chapter 2. A City Burns

1. Harrison, *Acres of Ashes*, 5.

2. Crooks, *Jacksonville after the Fire*, 12.

3. Foley and Wood, *The Great Fire of 1901*, 28.

4. Harrison, *Acres of Ashes*, 10–11.

5. Ibid., 12–13.

6. *Florida Times-Union*, May 4, 1901.

7. Ibid., 15.

8. Davis, *History of Jacksonville, Florida, and Vicinity*, 227.

9. *Savannah Morning News*, May 5, 1901.

10. Mencken, *Newspaper Days*, 94.

11. *Jacksonville Journal*, May 5, 1901.

12. *Florida Metropolis*, May 4, 1901.

13. *Savannah Morning News*, May 4, 1901.

14. Harrison, *Acres of Ashes*, 21.

15. Ibid., 30.

16. Smith, C., *Report of the Jacksonville Relief Association*, 12–18.

17. Mencken, *Newspaper Days*, 95.

18. Smith, C., *Report of the Jacksonville Relief Association*, 12–18.

19. Davis, *History of Jacksonville, Florida, and Vicinity*, 228.

20. *Florida Metropolis*, May 10, 1901.

21. Wood, *Jacksonville's Architectural Heritage*, 41.

22. *Florida Times-Union*, November 3, 1901.

23. Broward, *The Architecture of Henry John Klutho*, 21–23.

24. Ibid., 23.
25. Wood, *Jacksonville's Architectural Heritage*, 9.
26. *Florida Times-Union*, December 14, 1901.
27. Smith, C., *Jacksonville Board of Trade Report*, 86.
28. Crooks, *Jacksonville after the Fire*, 27.

Chapter 3. Kalem Comes to Town

1. Singer, "Manhattan Nickelodeons," 3–35.
2. Ezra, *Georges Méliès*, 8–9.
3. *Variety*, January 26, 1907, 12.
4. *Oakland Tribune*, July 11, 1908.
5. Balshofer and Miller, *One Reel a Week*, 5–9.
6. *Moving Picture World*, January 16, 1909, 57.
7. Bowser, *The Transformation of Cinema*, 41.
8. *Moving Picture World*, October 2, 1901, 57.
9. Ibid., January 9, 1909, 335.
10. Bowser, *The Transformation of Cinema*, 42.
11. Ibid.
12. Balshofer and Miller, *One Reel a Week*, 70.
13. Gauntier, "Blazing the Trail," 15–16, 132, 134.
14. Ibid.
15. Nelson, *Lights! Camera! Florida!* 13.
16. Gauntier, "Blazing the Trail," 15–16, 132, 134.
17. *Jacksonville and Florida Facts*, 11.
18. Gauntier, "Blazing the Trail," 15–16, 132, 134.
19. Ibid.
20. Ibid.
21. Nelson, *Lights! Camera! Florida!* 16.
22. Gauntier, "Blazing the Trail," 15–16, 132, 134.
23. Nelson, *Lights! Camera! Florida!* 18.
24. *New York Daily Mirror*, November 2, 1910.
25. Gauntier, "Blazing the Trail," 15–16, 132, 134.

Chapter 4. Meanwhile, on the West Coast . . .

1. www.usc.edu/libraries/archives/la.
2. Nelson, *Florida and the American Motion Picture Industry*, 71.

3. *Ciné-Journal*, October 11–18, 1909, 3–4.

4. Bowser, *The Transformation of Cinema*, 23.

5. Jacobs, *The Rise of the American Film*, 81–84.

6. Bowser, *The Transformation of Cinema*, 23.

7. Eyman, *The Speed of Sound*, 33.

8. Ramsaye, *A Million and One Nights*, 492.

9. Ibid., 498.

10. Sklar, *Movie-Made America*, 39.

11. Ramsaye, *A Million and One Nights*, 533.

12. Balshofer and Miller, *One Reel A Week*, 62.

13. Ibid., 64.

14. Sklar, *Movie-Made America*, 37.

15. Ibid., 36.

16. Wilson, 35.

17. Balshofer and Miller, *One Reel A Week*, 55.

18. Ibid., 54.

19. Horsley, "From Pigs to Pictures," Part One, 3.

20. Horsley, "From Pigs to Pictures," Part Two, 2.

21. Ibid., 2–3.

22. Ibid., 3.

Chapter 5. A Film Town Is Born

1. U.S. census data for years 1900–1920, reported in R. L. Polk & Co., *Florida State Gazetteer and Business Directory*, 1925, 37, 40.

2. Jacksonville Chamber of Commerce, *Jacksonville, Florida*, 1914.

3. *Florida Metropolis*, March 3, 1910.

4. Wood, *Jacksonville's Architectural Heritage*, 52.

5. Ibid., 68.

6. Nelson, *Florida and the American Motion Picture Industry*, 53.

7. *Motography*, May 16, 1914.

8. Nelson, *Florida and the American Motion Picture Industry*, 53.

9. Montgomery Amusement Company Prospectus, 1911, Film Archives, Jacksonville Historical Society.

10. Nelson, *Lights! Camera! Florida!* 13.

11. Ramsaye, *A Million and One Nights*, 507.

12. *New York Daily Mirror*, November 2, 1910.

13. Nelson, *Lights! Camera! Florida!* 19.

14. *Florida Times-Union*, February 18, 1910.

15. Nelson, *Florida and the American Motion Picture Industry*, 148.

16. Nelson, *Lights! Camera! Florida!* 20.

17. Nelson, *Florida and the American Motion Picture Industry*, 520.

18. Ibid., 541.

19. Ibid., 518.

20. Nelson, *Lights! Camera! Florida!*, 27.

21. *Florida Times-Union*, May 29, 1949.

22. Nelson, *Florida and the American Motion Picture Industry*, 514–41.

23. McCabe, *Babe: The Life of Oliver Hardy*, 16.

24. Ibid., 20.

25. Reitzhammer, "Jacksonville Titles."

26. Kalmus, "Technicolor Adventures in Cinemaland," 565.

27. Nelson, *Florida and the American Motion Picture Industry*, 534–35.

28. Kalmus, "Technicolor Adventures in Cinemaland," 566.

29. Letter from Frank H. Elmore to Dick Bussard, City Editor, *Jacksonville Journal*, October 6, 1971, Film Archives, Jacksonville Historical Society.

30. Duval Theatre program, Film Archives, Jacksonville Historical Society.

31. Ibid.

32. *Jacksonville Journal*, August 10, 1979.

33. Sklar, *Movie-Made America*, 69.

34. Nelson, *Lights! Camera! Florida!*, 26.

35. *Florida Times-Union*, January 12, 1916.

36. *Florida Times-Union*, July 5, 1916.

37. *Florida Metropolis*, September 9, 1916.

38. *Florida Times-Union*, July 5, 1916.

Chapter 6. The Movie Mayor

1. Gold, *History of Duval County, Florida*, 237.

2. Ibid.

3. Ibid.

4. Foley and Wood, *The Great Fire of 1901*, 141.

5. Ibid., 142.

6. Ibid., 141.

7. *Evening Telegraph*, November 16, 1893.

8. Cowart, *Crackers & Carpetbaggers*, 142.

9. Ibid., 143.

10. Ibid., 144.

11. Ibid., 144.

12. *Florida Times-Union*, January 17, 1894.

13. Cowart, *Crackers & Carpetbaggers*, 152.

14. Davis, *History of Jacksonville, Florida, and Vicinity*, 200.

15. Ibid.

16. *Florida Times-Union*, June 6, 1899.

17. Ibid.

18. Ibid.

19. *Florida Times-Union*, June 9, 1899.

20. *Florida Times-Union*, May 4, 1901.

21. *Florida Metropolis*, May 4, 1901.

22. *Jacksonville Journal*, May 4, 1901.

23. Mencken, *Newspaper Days*, 95–96.

24. Foley and Wood, *The Great Fire of 1901*, 142.

25. *Florida Times-Union*, January 12, 1916.

26. Ibid.

27. Ibid.

28. Ibid.

Chapter 7. The Boom Goes Boom

1. *Florida Times-Union*, June 26, 1916.

2. *Florida Metropolis*, September 9, 1916.

3. *Florida Metropolis*, May 29, 1916.

4. Davis, *History of Jacksonville, Florida, and Vicinity*, 254.

5. *Jacksonville Journal*, June 15, 1979.

6. Davis, *History of Jacksonville, Florida, and Vicinity*, 260–69.

7. Ibid., 278.

8. Ibid., 252.

9. Ibid., 270.

10. Nelson, *Lights! Camera! Florida!* 33.

11. Nelson, *Florida and the American Motion Picture Industry*, 179.

12. Nelson, *Lights! Camera! Florida!* 33.

13. *Florida Times-Union*, August 31, 1977.

14. Adams, *The Clarion*, 230–31.

15. *Florida Times-Union*, January 4, 1916.

16. Ibid.

17. Ibid.
18. Ibid.
19. Ibid.
20. Ibid.
21. Gold, *History of Duval County, Florida*, 480.
22. *Florida Times-Union*, January 21, 1917.
23. *Florida Times-Union*, February 4, 1917.
24. Ibid.
25. *Florida Times-Union*, February 5, 1917.
26. *Florida Times-Union*, February 7, 1917.
27. Davis, *History of Jacksonville, Florida, and Vicinity*, 165–80.
28. *Florida Times-Union*, January 12, 1916.
29. Davis, *History of Jacksonville, Florida, and Vicinity*, 272–73.
30. Ibid.
31. *Florida Metropolis*, January 12, 1917.
32. Broward, *The Architecture of Henry John Klutho*, 202.
33. *Florida Metropolis*, July 17, 1917.
34. *Florida Times-Union*, January 1, 1921.
35. Ibid.
36. Ibid.
37. *Time Magazine*, "Murray Garsson's Suckers," August 12, 1946.
38. *New York Times*, March 28, 1957.
39. Broward, *The Architecture of Henry John Klutho*, 249.

Chapter 8. Reel People

1. Cripps, *Slow Fade to Black*, 85.
2. www.memory.loc.gov. Farm Security Administration/Office of War Information.
3. Passi Kola advertisement, Richard E. Norman Collection, Lilly Library, Indiana University (hereafter Norman collection).
4. Norman Film Manufacturing Company, "Have You Talent?" brochure, Norman Collection.
5. Nelson, *Florida and the American Motion Picture Industry*, 433.
6. Norman Film Manufacturing Company, "Have You Talent?"
7. Ibid.
8. Ibid.
9. *Green Eyed Monster* publicity, Black Film Center/Archive, Indiana University.

10. Ibid.

11. *The Chicago Defender*, June 25, 1921.

12. H. G. Till to Richard Norman, February 23, 1921, Norman Collection.

13. R. E. Norman to John Owens, August 15, 1921, Norman Collection.

14. *The Bull-Dogger* poster, Black Film Center/Archive.

15. Klotman, *Frame by Frame*, 84.

16. Letter to Anita Bush, July 20, 1921, Norman Collection.

17. Letter from Anita Bush, September 11, 1921, Norman Collection.

18. Klotman, *Frame by Frame*, 127.

19. *The Crimson Skull* poster, Black Film Center/Archive, Indiana University.

20. Norman Laboratories letterhead, Norman Collection.

21. Norman Film Manufacturing Co. Sharing Contract, January 11, 1923, Norman Collection.

22. Press sheet for *The Crimson Skull*, Black Film Center/Archive, Indiana University.

23. Press sheet for *Regeneration*, Black Film Center/Archive, Indiana University.

24. Norman Film Manufacturing Company, "Have You Talent?"

25. State of New York Motion Picture Commission to Richard Norman, September 19, 1924, Norman Collection.

26. Nelson, *Florida and the American Motion Picture Industry*, 434.

27. Richard Norman to Clarence A. Brooks, June 12, 1923, Norman Collection.

28. Clarence A. Brooks to Richard Norman, June 26, 1923, Norman Collection.

29. Micheaux Film Corporation to Richard Norman, August 7, 1926, Norman Collection.

30. Western Feature Films to Richard Norman, March 29, 1923, Norman Collection.

31. Press sheet for *Who Shall Take My Life?*, Norman Collection.

32. *Florida Times-Union*, November 30, 1975.

33. D. Ireland Thomas to Richard Norman, January 15, 1926, Norman Collection.

34. Richard Norman to Bessie Coleman, February 8, 1926, Norman Collection.

35. Press sheet for *The Flying Ace*, Black Film Center/Archive.

36. Heroh Motion Picture Company of Liberia to Richard Norman, September 16, 1929, Norman Collection.

37. Eyman, *The Speed of Sound*, 242.

38. Jacobs, *The Rise of the American Film*, 299.

39. Camera Phone Co. form letter, Norman Collection.

40. Nelson, *Florida and the American Motion Picture Industry*, 424.

Chapter 9. The Industry Moves On

1. Sklar, *Movie-Made America*, 76–77.

2. Ibid., 76–78.

3. Eyman, *Lion of Hollywood*, 54–55.

4. Nelson, *Florida and the American Motion Picture Industry*, 464–65.

5. Ibid., 465.

6. Smith, P., 4.

7. Schickel, *D. W. Griffith*, 421.

8. Nelson, *Florida and the American Motion Picture Industry*, 412.

9. Ibid., 412–14.

10. D. W. Griffith to Everest Sewell, July 11, 1921, Florida Photographic Collection, Tallahassee, Florida.

11. Schickel, *D. W. Griffith*, 476.

12. Fleischer, *Out of the Inkwell*, 49–50.

13. Ibid., 51.

14. Ibid., 105.

15. Ibid., 93–98.

16. Ibid., 119–20.

17. Foglesong, *Married to the Mouse*, 2–3.

18. Richard Hubler, interview with Joe Fowler, vice president of Walt Disney Productions, July 23, 1962, Disney Archives, Burbank, California.

19. Foglesong, *Married to the Mouse*, 15.

20. Ibid., 48.

21. *Orlando Evening Star*, May 28, 1965.

22. *Orlando Evening Star*, October 29, 1965.

23. *New York Times*, February 3, 1967.

24. Walt Disney Productions, "Excerpts of Remarks by Governor Claude R. Kirk, Jr.," February 2, 1967, Disney Depository, Orlando Public Library, Orlando, Florida.

25. Foglesong, *Married to the Mouse*, 4.

26. Ibid., 5.

27. Figures provided by the Orlando/Orange County Convention and Visitors Bureau.

28. "Creaturefest," available at www.creaturefest.com.

29. Jacksonville Historical Society Archives, "The Man Who Created Kong," available at jaxhistory.com/archives.htm.

30. Eyman, *Lion of Hollywood*, 200.

31. *Florida Times-Union*, April 8, 1927.

32. The Florida Theatre, "History and Heritage," available at www.floridatheatre.com/about/history.php.

33. Richard Norman to South Miami Colored School, October 18, 1939, Norman Collection.

Chapter 10. Jacksonville: Act Three

1. *Jacksonville Journal*, November 4, 1976.

2. Ibid.

3. Mormino, *Land of Sunshine, State of Dreams*, 23.

4. *Florida Times-Union*, October 4, 1989

5. Ibid.

6. Ibid.

7. *Florida Times-Union*, June 12, 2001.

8. *Jacksonville Journal*, June 12, 1981.

9. *Florida Times-Union*, March 8, 1984.

10. Jacksonville Film and Television Office, "Film and Television Office," available at www.coj.net/Departments/Jacksonville+Economic+Development+Commission/Film+and+Television/The+Office.htm.

11. *Florida Times-Union*, January 22, 2000.

12. Jacksonville Film and Television Office, "Economic Impact," available at www.coj.net/Departments/Jacksonville+Economic+Development+Commission/Film+and+Television/The+Economic+Impact.htm.

13. Interview with Todd Roobin, December 10, 2004.

14. Interview with Ann Burt, August 5, 2006.

15. *Arlington Community Improvement Strategy for Old Town*, May 31, 2001, 1–3, pamphlet in author's possession.

16. Interview with Ann Burt, August 5, 2006.

17. Ibid.

18. Ibid.

19. Ibid.

20. "The Fabulous Years of Silent Filmmaking in Florida," 6.

21. Interview with Ann Burt, August 5, 2006.

22. Interview with Devon Stuart, June 26, 2006.

23. Ibid.

24. Ibid.

25. Old Arlington, Inc., monthly newsletter, January 2007, in author's possession.

26. Time Warner, "Fact Sheet," available at www.timewarner.com/corp/aboutus/fact_sheet.html (accessed February 24, 2007).

27. Governor's Office of Film and Entertainment, "Governor Crist Recommends $75 Million For Florida's Entertainment Industry Financial Incentive," available at www.filminflorida.com/wh/ViewNewsItem.asp?id=490.

28. Los Angeles Convention and Visitors Bureau, "L.A. Travel Stats 2006," available at www.laincresearch.com/all/LATravelStats06Final.pdf.

29. Jacksonville Economic Development Commission, "Downtown Projects," available at www.coj.net/Departments/Jacksonville+Economic+Development+Commission/Downtown+Development/Downtown+Projects.htm.

Bibliography

Adams, Samuel Hopkins. *The Clarion*. New York: Houghton Mifflin Company, 1914. Reprint. Rockville, Md.: Wildside Press, 2005.

Akin, Edward N. *Flagler: Rockefeller Partner and Florida Baron*. Jacksonville: University Press of Florida, 1991.

Balshofer, Fred J., and Arthur C. Miller. *One Reel a Week*. London: Cambridge University Press, 1967.

Bowser, Eileen. *The Transformation of Cinema, 1907–1915*. Berkeley and Los Angeles: University of California Press, 1990.

Broward, Robert C. *The Architecture of Henry John Klutho: The Prairie School in Jacksonville*. Jacksonville: University of North Florida Press, 1983.

Cowart, John W. *Crackers & Carpetbaggers: Moments in the History of Jacksonville, Florida*. Jacksonville: Bluefish Books, 2005.

Cripps, Thomas. *Slow Fade to Black: The Negro in American Film, 1900–1942*. Bloomington: Indiana University Press, 1978.

———. "The Birth of a Race Company: An Early Stride Toward a Black Cinema." *Journal of Negro History* 59, no. 1 (January 1974): 28–37.

Crooks, James B. *Jacksonville after the Fire, 1901–1919: A New South City*. Gainesville: University Press of Florida, 1991.

Davis, T. Frederick. *History of Jacksonville, Florida, and Vicinity, 1513 to 1924*. St. Augustine: Florida Historical Society, 1925.

Eliade, Mircea. *Shamanism: Archaic Techniques of Ecstasy*. Princeton, N.J.: Princeton University Press, 1972.

Eyman, Scott. *Lion of Hollywood: The Life and Legend of Louis B. Mayer*. New York: Simon & Schuster, 2005.

Ezra, Elizabeth. *Georges Méliès*. New York: St. Martin's Press, 2000.

———. *The Speed of Sound: Hollywood and the Talkie Revolution, 1926–1930*. Baltimore, Md.: Johns Hopkins University Press, 1997.

"The Fabulous Years of Silent Filmmaking in Florida." *The Cummer Magazine* (August-September-October 2004): 4–6.

Fleischer, Richard. *Out of the Inkwell: Max Fleischer and the Animation Revolution*. Lexington: University Press of Kentucky, 2005.

Foglesong, Richard E. *Married to the Mouse: Walt Disney World and Orlando*. New Haven, Conn.: Yale University Press, 2001.

Foley, Bill, and Wayne W. Wood. *The Great Fire of 1901*. Jacksonville: Jacksonville Historical Society, the Hartley Press, 2001.

Fry, Gladys-Marie. *Night Riders in Black Folk History*. Athens: University of Georgia Press, 1975.

Gauntier, Gene. "Blazing the Trail." *Woman's Home Companion* (November 1928): 15–16, 132, 134.

Gold, Pleasant Daniel. *History of Duval County, Florida*. St. Augustine: The Record Company, 1928.

Hakluyt, Richard. *The Voyages, Traffiques, and Discoveries of Foreign Voyagers*. New York: E. P. Dutton & Company, 1928.

Harrison, Benjamin. *Acres of Ashes*. Jacksonville: James A. Holloman, 1901.

Horsley, David. "From Pigs to Pictures: The Story of David Horsley." Part 1. *The International Photographer* (March 1934): 2–3.

———. "From Pigs to Pictures: The Story of David Horsley." Part 2. *The International Photographer* (April 1934): 2–3.

Howe, Joseph W. *Winter Homes for Invalids: An Account of the Various Localities in Europe and America, Suitable for Consumptives and Other Invalids during the Winter Months, with Special Reference to the Climactic Variations at Each Place, and Their Influence on Disease*. New York: G. T. Putnam's Sons, 1875.

J. Wiggins & Co. *Jacksonville Directory for 1900*. Jacksonville: J. Wiggins & Co., 1900.

Jacksonville Chamber of Commerce. *Jacksonville, Florida*. Jacksonville: Arnold Printing Company, 1914.

Jacobs, Lewis. *The Rise of the American Film: A Critical History*. New York: Teachers College, Columbia University, 1974.

Kalmus, Herbert. "Technicolor Adventures in Cinemaland." *Journal of the Society of Motion Picture Engineers* (December 1938): 564–85.

Klotman, Phyllis Rauch. *Frame by Frame—A Black Filmography*. Bloomington: Indiana University Press, 1979.

Martin, Richard A. *Consolidation: Jacksonville Duval County; The Dynamics of Urban Political Reform*. Jacksonville: Crawford Publishing Co., 1968.

McCabe, John. *Babe: The Life of Oliver Hardy*. New York: Citadel Press, 1989.

Mencken, H. L. *Newspaper Days: 1899–1906*. New York: Knopf, 1941.

Mormino, Gary N. *Land of Sunshine, State of Dreams: A Social History of Modern Florida*. Gainesville: University Press of Florida, 2005.

"Murray Garsson's Suckers." *Time*, August 12, 1946. Available at http://www.time.com/time/magazine/article/0,9171,793133,00.html.

Nelson, Richard Alan. *Florida and the American Motion Picture Industry, 1898–1980*. 2 vols. New York: Garland Publishing, 1983.

Newton, Michael. *The Invisible Empire: The Ku Klux Klan in Florida*. Gainesville: University Press of Florida, 2001.

———. *Lights! Camera! Florida! Ninety Years of Moviemaking and Television Production in the Sunshine State*. Tampa: Florida Endowment for the Humanities, 1987.

R. L. Polk and Company. *Florida State Gazetteer and Business Directory*. Jacksonville: R. L. Polk and Company, 1925.

———. *Jacksonville City Directory*. Jacksonville: R. L. Polk and Company, 1915.

Ramsaye, Terry. *A Million and One Nights*. New York: Simon & Schuster, 1926.

Rawls, Oscar G. "Ninety-Six Years of Engineering Development on the St. Johns River." *Jacksonville Historical Society Papers* 2 (1949): 45–61.

Reitzhammer, John B. "Jacksonville Titles." Compiled December 9, 1986. Film Collection at the Celeste Bartos Film Preservation Center, Museum of Modern Art Film Study Center, New York.

Rittaud-Hutinet, Jacques. *Letters: Auguste and Louis Lumière*. London: Faber and Faber Limited, 1995.

Schickel, Richard. *D. W. Griffith: An American Life*. New York: Simon and Schuster, 1984.

Singer, Ben. "Manhattan Nickelodeons: New Data on Audiences and Exhibitors." *Cinema Journal* (Spring 1995): 5–35.

Sklar, Robert. *Movie-Made America: A Cultural History of American Movies*. New York: Random House, 1974.

Smith, Charles H. *Jacksonville and Florida Facts*. Jacksonville: Jacksonville Board of Trade, 1906.

————. *Jacksonville Board of Trade Report*. Jacksonville: Garrett Printing Company, 1902.

————. *Report of the Jacksonville Relief Association*. Jacksonville: Jacksonville Relief Association, 1901.

Smith, Patrick D. *A Land Remembered*. Sarasota: Pineapple Press, 1984.

Ward, James Robertson. *Old Hickory's Town: An Illustrated History of Jacksonville*. Jacksonville: Florida Publishing Company, 1982.

Wilson, Woodrow. *The New Freedom: A Call for the Emanicipation of the Generous Energies of a People*. New York and Garden City: Doubleday and Page Co., 1918.

Wood, Wayne W. *Jacksonville's Architectural Heritage: Landmarks for the Future*. Jacksonville: Jacksonville Historical Landmarks Commission, University of North Florida Press, 1989.

Collections

Black Film Center/Archive, Indiana University, Bloomington, Indiana

Cummer Museum of Art and Gardens, Jacksonville, Florida

Disney Archives, Burbank, California

Disney Depository, Orlando Public Library, Orlando, Florida

Florida Photographic Collection, Tallahassee, Florida

Jacksonville Historical Society, Jacksonville, Florida

Museum of Florida History, Florida Department of State, Tallahassee, Florida

Museum of Modern Art Film Study Center, New York, New York

Norman Studios Silent Film Museum, Jacksonville, Florida

Richard E. Norman Collection, Lilly Library, Indiana University, Bloomington, Indiana

Web Sites

"Creaturefest." Available at www.creaturefest.com, accessed August 24, 2006.

The Florida Theatre. "History and Heritage." Available at www.floridatheatre.com/about/history.php, accessed April 7, 2006.

Governor's Office of Film and Entertainment. "Governor Crist Recommends $75 Million For Florida's Entertainment Industry Financial Incentive." Available at www.filminflorida.com/wh/ViewNewsItem.asp?id=490, accessed February 3, 2007.

Jacksonville Economic Development Commission. "Downtown Projects." Available at www.coj.net/Departments/Jacksonville+Economic+Development+Commission/Downtown+Development/Downtown+Projects.htm, accessed February 9, 2007.

Jacksonville Film and Television Office. "Economic Impact." Available at www.coj.net/Departments/Jacksonville+Economic+Development+Commission/Film+and+Television/The+Economic+Impact.htm, accessed January 31, 2007.

Jacksonville Film and Television Office. "Film and Television Office." Available at www.coj.net/Departments/Jacksonville+Economic+Development+Commission/Film+and+Television/The+Office.htm, accessed January 31, 2007.

Jacksonville Historical Society Archives. "The Man Who Created Kong." Available at jaxhistory.com/archives.htm, accessed May 12, 2006.

Library of Congress. "Farm Security Administration/Office of War Information Photograph Collection." Available at www.memory.loc.gov, accessed February 17, 2007.

Los Angeles Convention and Visitors Bureau. "L.A. Travel Stats 2006." Available at www.laincresearch.com/all/LATravelStats06Final.pdf, accessed February 4, 2007.

Los Angeles: Past, Present and Future. University of Southern California Library Archives. "Father Crespi in Los Angeles." Available at www.usc.edu/libraries/archives/la, accessed January 26, 2007.

Time Warner. "Fact Sheet." Available at www.timewarner.com/corp/aboutus/fact_sheet.html, accessed February 24, 2007.

Index